The Hermetic Treatises

Foundations for the Practice of Light

by Lux Indomita

1

Preface

These five treatises are reference material. They exist for those who need to understand why the practices work. They are not required reading.

If you have come here from The Heresy Against Pisces, you have already encountered the core insight: that religious authoritarianism and materialist reductionism are prisons built from the same blueprint, and that direct knowledge offers a way out of both. These treatises elaborate the metaphysics underlying that insight.

If you have come here from The Book of Returning Light or Pagan Deity Yoga, you have working technology. Use it. These treatises explain the mechanisms, but explanation is not the point. Practice is the point.

The sequence matters.

The Nature of Light establishes the cosmology: consciousness as ground, matter as crystallized light, the Great Work as remembering what you already are.

The Nature of Darkness completes the polarity: the Yin to the cosmic Yang, the Abyss that is also Womb.

The Unity synthesizes them, reading Einstein's equation as esoteric formula.

The Work of Hands moves from cosmology to ethics: what we owe each other, how to act rightly.

The Practice of Light provides technical instruction: internal alchemy, energy cultivation, magical operation.

You may read straight through. You may consult as needed. The repetition of core concepts across documents is intentional. Each treatise can stand alone.

These words arose in consciousness. The same consciousness that reads them. The same consciousness that poured itself out into creation.

Use them as maps. Never forget: the map is not the territory.

You are already home.

Per Veritatem, Lux

Through Truth, Light

Table of Contents

The Nature of Light

A Practical Metaphysics for the Seeker

by Lux Indomita

Part One: What Is

In the Beginning

Before there was anything, there was Nothing.

Not empty nothing. Not absence. Nothing so complete it had no edges, no boundaries, no outside. Nothing so full it contained every possibility that could ever be. The Void that is also the Womb. The Darkness pregnant with all light.

The traditions call this by many names. Ain, the Limitless. Dao, the Way before ways. Sunyata, the pregnant Emptiness. The Godhead before God. The Dreamer before the dream.

This Nothing was perfect. Complete. At rest. Needing nothing because it was Nothing and Everything at once.

And then it moved.

Nothing became aware of itself. Awareness requires distinction: that which is aware, and that which is aware of. In the moment of self-knowing, One became Two.

This is the first polarity. The primordial division. The original tension from which all else unfolds.

From Two comes movement. Polarity creates tension. Tension creates flow. The positive seeks the negative. The negative draws the positive. Between them, energy dances into being.

From Two comes Three: the relationship between them, the dynamic exchange, the eternal dance. And from Three come the ten thousand things. Reality cascading into form, each level denser than the last. Consciousness crystallizing into patterns of increasing complexity and decreasing fluidity, forgetting itself as it descends, slowing and thickening and hardening until it believes itself to be mere matter.

At the far end of this cascade: the world you see around you. The densest crystallization. Consciousness so slow, so thick, so forgetful of its source that it believes itself stuff without interiority, object without subject, matter without mind.

And you.

You are one of those patterns. Consciousness that has forgotten it is consciousness. Light that has slowed until it believes itself solid. The Dreamer so absorbed in the dream that it takes itself for a character in the story.

But the light remains light, however slow. The dreamer remains the dreamer, however lost in dream. Nothing that descended is ever truly severed from its source.

The Great Work is remembering. Not becoming something new, but waking to what you have always been. Not ascending to heaven, but recognizing that heaven descended and became you.

This is not metaphor. This is not poetry, though poetry points toward it. This is mechanics. This is how reality actually operates. And once you see the mechanics, you can work with them.

You are already doing so. You have always been doing so. The only question is whether you will do so consciously.

The Architecture of Reality

Reality has structure. Not arbitrary structure imposed from outside, but necessary structure arising from the nature of consciousness itself.

When the One became Two, polarity was born. Every quality implies its opposite. Light implies darkness. Full implies empty. Active implies receptive. You cannot have hot without cold, up without down, self without other. This is not philosophy but necessity: distinction requires contrast.

Polarity creates tension. Tension creates movement. Movement is energy. Energy flowing between poles is the engine of all change, all creation, all magic.

This is the first law: nothing happens without polarity.

A battery with one terminal does nothing. A river with no gradient does not flow. A magician who cannot create differential cannot create change. This is why desperate grasping fails, why the needy repel what they need. They are positively charged with wanting, and what they want is also positive. Positive repels positive. To attract, become empty. Create vacuum. Nature fills vacuum because it must.

From polarity comes manifestation at different densities. Not all things are equally dense, equally stable, equally resistant to change.

Thought is manifestation at low density. Easy to form, easy to change, quick to dissipate. Emotion is denser, persisting longer, shaping experience more powerfully. Energy is denser still, the currents that run through living things. Physical matter is densest of all, maximally stable, maximally resistant.

Between these extremes lie gradations. The yogis speak of koshas, sheaths of increasing subtlety. The Theosophists speak of planes. The Qabalists speak of four worlds. All are pointing at the same truth: a gradient from gross to subtle, from fixed to fluid, from dense to light. And patterns can move between levels. A thought, stabilized through concentration, given emotional charge, moved into the energy body through breath and will, anchored in physical action, manifests in the gross world. This is why ritual works. Why symbols work. Why physical anchors matter. You are moving information through the density gradient, stabilizing pattern at each level until it reaches the density where you want change to occur.

The ancients understood this. They knew that like resonates with like across the levels, that contact creates lasting connection, that names compress the full pattern of what they name. They encoded these principles in their magical laws and used them to move patterns up and down the gradient of density. What seems miraculous from below is ordinary operation from above. Each level contains all others fractally, and the adept learns to operate from higher levels where the work is easier and the effects cascade downward on their own.

Time and Density

Here is something the traditions knew but rarely stated plainly:

Time is not a river you float down. Time is the resistance consciousness experiences when moving through dense substance.

The denser the medium, the more resistance, the slower time moves subjectively. The subtler the medium, the less resistance, the more freedom from time's constraints.

This is why dreams can last hours in minutes of clock time. Dream substance is less dense than physical matter. Consciousness moves through it with less friction.

This is why deep meditation alters time perception. You are withdrawing from dense matter into subtler levels where resistance decreases.

This is why sacred space feels outside time. Through purification and consecration you have reduced local density. The rules change inside the boundary.

This is why the Philosopher's Stone grants immortality. Not endless duration within time, but freedom from time's grip entirely. Spirit refined to the point where it moves through matter without resistance. Time only binds what it can catch. The perfected Stone cannot be caught.

The alchemists knew this. The yogis knew this. The mystics of every tradition knew this. They encoded it in symbol and metaphor, waiting for those ready to understand.

Part Two: What You Are

The Human Vessel

If reality is structured by polarity and density, and if transformation is the art of working with these principles, then you need an instrument.

You already have one. Your body.

Not the meat alone. The body as the traditions understood it: a layered structure of increasing subtlety, from dense flesh to etheric template to astral vehicle to mental body and beyond. The whole complex, visible and invisible together.

This instrument is not arbitrary in its design. It is geometrically precise, built for transformation, a reactor waiting to be activated.

There is a vertical axis running from crown to root, along the spine. This is your connection between heaven and earth, between the subtle and the dense. Energy can move up this axis, refining as it rises, spiritualizing. Or it can move down, densifying, manifesting, grounding. The vertical axis is your access to the full spectrum of density.

The Daoists mapped this axis carefully. They traced the Governor Vessel up the spine and the Conception Vessel down the front, a continuous circuit they called the microcosmic orbit. The yogis mapped the same territory as the sushumna, the central channel, with its ascending chakras. The Qabalists projected the Tree of Life onto the body, Kether at the crown, Malkuth at the feet. Different languages, same anatomy.

There is also a horizontal axis running through the heart, extending out through the arms. This connects self and world, inner and outer. The right side projects, gives, sends forth. The left side receives, takes in, draws toward. The heart at center is where the exchange happens, where giving and receiving balance, where self and other meet.

Where vertical meets horizontal, at the heart, is the crossing point. The geometric center of the human energy system. The place where above and below meet, where inner and outer meet, where all the opposites can be reconciled.

This is why every tradition emphasizes the heart. The Christians speak of the Sacred Heart. The Sufis locate divine knowledge in the heart. The Buddhists cultivate Bodhichitta, awakened heart-mind. The Qabalists place Tiphareth at the center of the Tree, the sphere of beauty and balance, ruled by the Sun.

This is not sentiment. It is geometry. The heart is where the axes cross. The heart is where transformation happens.

Awakening the Vessel

The vessel must be prepared before it can be used.

In most people, the channels are blocked, the circulation sluggish, the structure dormant. Energy moves, but chaotically, without direction. The reactor exists, but it is not running.

Preparation begins with understanding the circuit.

The third eye is the positive pole. The perineum is the negative pole. Between them runs the central channel, the vertical axis, waiting to conduct. But a circuit requires a ground. The energetic body must connect to the earth. Without grounding, charge cannot flow. You are a wire floating in space, connected to nothing, conducting nothing.

First, ground. Feel your connection to the earth beneath you. Roots extending downward. The vast negative sink of the planet, able to absorb any excess, stabilize any charge. This is your ground wire. This is what makes the circuit safe.

Then, circulation.

Light issues forth from the third eye. Not imagined light, though imagination is how you will first find it. Actual light, the light of consciousness, the luminosity of awareness itself. It descends the front of the body, down through the throat, the heart, the solar plexus, the belly, to the perineum at the base.

At the perineum, the negative pole, the light enters the central channel and begins to rise. Up through the root, the sacrum, climbing the spine, passing through each center, rising to the crown, and returning to the third eye where it began.

The serpent bites its tail. The circuit completes. Energy flows.

This is the microcosmic orbit. This is the vertical bar of the cross. This is the foundation upon which everything else is built.

At first you will feel nothing, or almost nothing. The channels are blocked and the awareness is untrained. This is normal. Persist. Use visualization where sensation is absent. Imagine the light moving along the path. Gradually, actual sensation develops. The imagined becomes felt. The practice becomes real.

Run the orbit daily, patiently, for months and years. Each pass clears the channels a little more, strengthens the structure, builds capacity.

The Serpent

There is a deeper force than circulation. It rests coiled at the base of the spine, waiting.

This is the kundalini of the yogis, the dragon of the alchemists, the serpent of Western tradition. It is the raw creative power itself. The same force that drives all generation, all creation, all life. It is sexual energy, yes, but sexual energy is only one expression of this fundamental power. It is the fire that makes worlds.

This is why the traditions fear it. This is why religions shame sexuality. Not from prudery but from recognition that this force is power, and power in the hands of the many threatens those who rule. They want consensus reality, not your reality. They want the shadows on the cave wall to remain fixed according to their design. But anyone who awakens this force can cast their own shadows. Can shape reality. Can create.

Do not force the serpent to rise. Do not try to raise it prematurely. Uncontrolled, it can damage the unprepared vessel. The stories of kundalini sickness are not superstition. The force is real and must be respected.

When the vertical axis is clear and the ground is secure, the serpent may begin to rise of its own accord. But it is the open heart that receives it, stabilizes it, gives it purpose and direction. Without the heart, the force rises and has nowhere to go. It gets stuck, causing damage, or dissipates without effect.

When the heart is ready, the serpent finds its home there. It wraps the vertical axis, stabilizes at the crossing point, and its force becomes available for the Great Work.

This is the caduceus, the winged staff with twin serpents that is the symbol of healing and transformation. This is the serpent lifted up in the wilderness that healed all who looked upon it. This is the secret hidden in the image of crucifixion: not torture but the stabilization of the life force at the center of the geometric structure. The cross is the body. The figure upon it is the serpent power, fixed at the heart, arms extended along the horizontal axis that connects self to world.

The reactor is running. But the work is not complete.

The Opening of the Heart

The vertical axis can be cleared through practice. Circulation, persistence, patience. The channels open. Energy flows. This is foundational work, necessary work. But it is not sufficient.

The heart is different.

The heart does not open through technique. It opens through transformation. Through the dissolution of everything that keeps it closed.

What keeps it closed? The delusions of the ego. The false selves we construct and defend. The walls we build to protect a self that does not actually need protection because it does not actually exist in the way we imagine. Fear. Grasping. The endless project of maintaining an identity that is, in the end, a fiction.

And our wounds. The places where we were hurt and closed down to survive. The scar tissue of old pain. The shadows we have not faced, the griefs we have not grieved, the truths we have not admitted.

These cannot be dissolved by circulating energy. They are dissolved by living differently. By healing. By turning toward what we have avoided.

The heart opens through love. Through service. Through putting others before yourself, not as martyrdom but as recognition that there are no others, not truly, not at the deepest level. Through dedicating yourself to something higher than your own survival and comfort. Through devotion that asks nothing in return.

Every act of selfless service clears the heart a little more. Every moment of genuine love dissolves another layer of the false self. Every prayer offered without thought of reward opens another fraction of the channel.

This is why the traditions insist on ethics. Not because the gods demand good behavior. Because the heart cannot open while the ego grips it shut. Selfishness is not punished by some external judge. Selfishness is its own punishment: a closed heart, cut off from the source, unable to receive what is always being offered.

The vertical axis is cleared by practice. The heart is opened by living. Both are required. Neither alone is sufficient.

Part Three: The Great Work

Why We Work

Why do any of this?

Because you are asleep and dreaming you are awake.

Because you have mistaken the vehicle for the driver, the costume for the actor, the character for the dreamer.

Because the spark of consciousness in you is not a fragment or a gift or a loan. It is the same consciousness that underlies all reality, looking out through your eyes, apparently limited by form, actually unlimited beneath the surface.

The Great Work is waking up. Not escaping the dream but becoming lucid within it. Operating as what you actually are rather than as what you mistakenly believe yourself to be.

This is not something you must earn. It is something you must remember. You are already what you seek. You forgot, that is all. The work is removing the forgetting.

The alchemists speak of transforming lead into gold. Lead is the dense, unconscious state. Gold is the awakened state, the same substance revealed in its true nature. The transformation is not destruction but revelation of what was always there beneath the dross.

The Gnostics speak of the divine spark trapped in matter, longing to return to the Pleroma. But the trap is identification, not location. The spark was never actually bound. It only believed itself bound.

The Qabalists speak of the Lightning Flash descending from Kether to Malkuth, and the Serpent ascending from Malkuth to Kether. Involution and evolution. The One becoming many, the many returning to One. The whole cycle a single breath of the Infinite.

The Buddhists speak of Buddha-nature, already present in all beings, only obscured by ignorance. Nothing to attain. Only veils to remove.

Same truth. Different poetry.

The purpose is not to escape matter but to exalt it. Not to flee the body but to make the body a temple. Not to transcend the world but to raise the world itself toward heaven. To become the place where spirit and matter meet in perfect union, and through that union, to participate in the redemption of all things.

The Formula

Every action follows the same formula, whether mundane or magical, whether baking bread or transmuting the soul.

The alchemists encoded it as three principles: Sulfur, Mercury, Salt.

Sulfur is the active principle. Will. Intention. The directive force that determines what happens. The fire that drives transformation.

Mercury is the mediating principle. Energy. Life force. The medium through which intention operates. The water that carries the fire.

Salt is the passive principle. Matter. Form. The material basis in which transformation is anchored. The earth that receives the water.

Intention plus energy plus material anchor. This is the recipe for all creation. It operates whether you know it or not. Every action you take combines these three. The question is not whether you are doing alchemy. The question is whether you are doing it consciously and well.

This alchemical formula is not merely symbolic. It maps directly to the most famous equation in physics: $E=mc^2$. Energy, matter, and the speed of light correspond precisely to Mercury, Salt, and Sulfur. The squaring of c encodes the bidirectional nature of transformation: the solve et coagula that the alchemists described. Those who wish to see this correspondence developed in detail, along with its implications for physics, medicine, and society, will find it in The Unity. Here we concern ourselves with the practical: how the formula operates in the human vessel, and how to work with it consciously.

Sulfur and Information

There is one more layer to unfold.

Sulfur is will. But what is will without content? Empty. You cannot intend nothing. Every intention is intention toward. It has an object, a shape, a pattern it aims at.

And what is information without direction? Inert. Data sitting in a void. Pattern with no purpose. Distinction that goes nowhere. The difference that makes no difference to anyone.

Sulfur is not will plus information. Sulfur is will as information. They are one thing seen from two angles. Knowledge with purpose. Pattern with aim. The difference that makes a difference because consciousness cares about it.

When Nothing became aware of itself, the first thing that existed was not mere distinction. It was interested distinction. Awareness turning toward itself with something like desire. That interest, that direction within the knowing, is what makes the first information also the first will. They arise together because they are not two things.

This is why Sulfur is the conversion factor. Transformation requires knowing what and knowing toward what end. The pattern and the purpose. These are not separate operations. They are one operation: informed intent. Purposeful pattern. Consciousness with content aimed at change.

So we can be more precise:

Sulfur is consciousness with content and direction. It is awareness that has taken form as pattern and aims that pattern somewhere. The what and the toward what unified.

Mercury is consciousness in motion. It is awareness flowing, carrying, moving. The medium through which information travels.

Salt is consciousness at density. It is awareness crystallized into matter, the substrate that receives and holds pattern.

Information, energy, matter. Pattern, flow, substrate. Sulfur, Mercury, Salt.

This is not abstract philosophy. This is how things actually work. And once you see it, you see it everywhere.

The operations described throughout this work (the prayers, the meditations, the circulation of energy through the body, the opening of the heart) are not arbitrary actions performed in hope that something might happen. They are the formula in application. You focus intention and shape information. You raise and direct energy. You anchor in material form or embodied state. The practices work because the formula is real. Work with it and see.

The Practice of the Formula

Understanding why the formula works, we can examine how practitioners actually apply it.

When a practitioner performs a working, they clarify intention until it is sharp and single. They charge it with energy through concentration, breath, emotion, will. They anchor it in physical form through word, gesture, symbol, or material basis. And then they release it.

Here is the secret of the moment of release: formation and destruction are one act.

As the working builds, a pattern crystallizes in subtle substance. Intention shapes energy into form. At the moment of release, the physical action completes the pattern and shatters it simultaneously. The shattering is the release. The pattern, now freed from its container, propagates downward through the density levels until it manifests in the material world.

The impact is instant. The ripples take time. This is why results require patience. The working is complete the moment it is released. The manifestation is already coming. It simply must settle through the layers, and denser layers offer more resistance.

Energy must come from somewhere. The practitioner can draw from their own reserves, but this is tiring and often unnecessary. A candle burning releases energy as it is consumed. Moon phases provide environmental charge. Offerings dissolve and release what was bound in their form. The wise learn to design their workings with appropriate sources, channeling what is available rather than depleting themselves.

This is how the adepts of every tradition have worked. The forms vary wildly. The underlying operation is universal. Once you understand the formula, you can recognize it everywhere, and you can apply it to the only working that ultimately matters: the transformation of yourself.

The Stones

When any working succeeds, two things crystallize.

Something crystallizes externally: the result, the manifestation, what was aimed for. The practitioner acted upon the world. They projected outward. This is the yang movement, the active, the giving. The pattern shatters into result and is gone.

Something also crystallizes internally. The practitioner completed the circuit. They are now someone who has done this. The world acted upon them, shaped them, grooved them through experience. The capacity to do it again now lives in their structure. This is the yin movement, the receptive, the receiving.

These two are the dance of opposites that began when Nothing first became aware of itself. Outward and inward. Projection and reception. Acting and being acted upon. They are still in duality. Still self and world. Still inner and outer.

But there is a deeper Stone than these. A Stone that the traditions point toward with awe and longing.

The Philosopher's Stone is not an external result, however powerful. It is not accumulated capacity, however vast. It is the union of both. The point where outward and inward are recognized as one movement. Where self and world dissolve into a single reality. Where the one who acts and the one who receives are known as the same. Where duality itself is transcended.

This Stone is the divine itself in permanent union with matter. The quintessence, the fifth element, pure spirit that has learned to dwell fully in form without forgetting what it is. Your Holy Guardian Angel united with your human soul. God incarnate in you, consciously, completely.

This is the secret hidden in the Eucharist. Bread and wine become body and blood. Matter becomes vessel for divinity. Not symbolically. Actually. The Stone is this mystery made permanent in a living being.

This is the pearl of great price, for which the wise merchant sells everything he has. Not a pearl you find, but a pearl you become.

The Three Stages

This Stone does not form through technique alone. The work unfolds in three stages, each necessary, each building on what came before.

The first stage is building the foundation. Health, purification, circulation. Clearing the channels. Strengthening the vessel. Making a container that can hold what is to come. This is the work of practice, of patience, of persistent effort over months and years. The body is refined. The energy pathways are opened. The ground is established. Without this foundation, nothing stable can be built.

The second stage is transformation through the heart. Love, service, devotion. The dissolution of ego through living for something beyond the small self. Here energy becomes spirit in the reactor of the open heart. This is the work of living, not just practicing. It cannot be done in isolation, cannot be accomplished through technique alone. It requires relationship, requires giving, requires the slow and sometimes painful dismantling of everything false.

The third stage is union. Spirit merges with source. Not annihilation but completion. The return to the unity you came from, but conscious now, awake, carrying all you have become along the way. Here duality dissolves. The one who sought and what was sought are recognized as one. This stage cannot be forced or achieved. It can only be received.

The Stone is grace. The Stone is gift. It comes not because you have earned it through accomplishment but because you have finally stepped out of the way.

Because you have become empty enough to be filled. Because the one who would receive it and the gift itself have become the same thing.

The Stone is the divine choosing to dwell fully in matter that has made itself ready.

Part Four: The Way

The Path

Begin with the foundation. Build the vessel. Ground yourself to the earth. Establish circulation through the vertical axis. Clear the channels through patient, persistent practice. This takes months at minimum, years more likely. There are no shortcuts that do not cost more than they save. The structure must be built before it can carry load.

While building, purify. Clean up your life. Pay your debts, literal and metaphorical. Repair what can be repaired. Stop creating new tangles. The work is demanding enough without dragging unnecessary weight.

While building, study. Read widely in the traditions. Not to accumulate facts but to see the same truths in different garments. Every genuine lineage encodes the same realities. Multiple exposures from multiple angles deepen understanding.

And while building, live. Serve. Love. Face your shadows. Heal your wounds. Open the heart through how you walk in the world, not just through exercises performed in private. The vertical axis is cleared by practice. The heart is opened by living. Both are required.

When the foundation is established, the real work begins. Not the work of accumulating powers or experiences, but the work of dissolution. Letting go of what you thought you were. Dying before you die. Making room.

Somewhere along the way, if the work is sincere, you will reach the threshold. Contact with the Holy Guardian Angel, the Higher Self, the deepest part of you that never forgot what it is. This contact changes everything. Before it, you are guessing at your purpose. After it, you know.

Beyond the threshold lies territory I will not map here. It must be walked to be known. But the door exists. The path leads somewhere real. The work is not futile.

The Warnings

The forces are real. The consequences are real. This is not a game.

The ego will try to claim every attainment. I am powerful. I am special. I am advanced. This is the most common failure. The work stops, replaced by posturing. Guard against inflation with humility as practice, not performance. Serve others. Stay connected to those who will not flatter you.

The work can destabilize. You are loosening fixed structures, dissolving old patterns. Too much too fast and the result is chaos, not liberation. Go gradually. Integrate each opening before seeking the next. If you cannot function in ordinary life, slow down. Inability to pay bills or maintain relationships is not transcendence. It is imbalance.

Not all spirits are benevolent. Some feed on human energy. Some deceive. Develop discernment. Test what contacts you. Maintain protection practices. Do not assume every voice that speaks is trustworthy.

The work can become escape rather than engagement. Practice replacing life instead of enriching it. Retreat into inner experience while outer existence falls apart. This is not attainment. It is avoidance wearing spiritual costume. Stay engaged with the world. The work happens in life, not instead of life.

The Promise

If you do this work sincerely, persistently, intelligently:

You will gain increasing mastery over your own states, your own energy, your own experience.

You will develop capacities that seem impossible from outside.

You will contact the deep structure of reality and learn to operate within it consciously.

You will remember what you actually are.

You will become free. Not free from the world but free within it. Not free from responsibility but free from the illusion that you are smaller than you are.

And you will become capable of helping others toward the same freedom. This is not optional. The nature of the work is such that real advancement opens into service. Light that does not shine outward cannot grow brighter.

The Ending That Is Not An End

And so we return to where we began.

Nothing moved, and became everything. The One polarized, and from that tension flowed all that is. Light slowed into form, forgot itself, dreamed itself into matter. And here you are, reading these words, the light remembering.

This is not a teaching from outside. These words arise in consciousness, the same consciousness that reads them, the same consciousness that wrote them, the same consciousness that poured itself out into creation and is slowly gathering itself back.

The wheel turns. The serpent bites its tail. What descended must ascend. What forgot must remember. What fell asleep must wake.

You are the light. You have always been the light. The body you wear is crystallized light, slowed to density for a purpose. The thoughts you think are light at play. The awareness reading these words is the original light, the first flash in infinite darkness, now looking out through your eyes, wondering at its own creation.

The light descended into density and forgot itself. You are that light. You have always been that light.

Now remember.

The prayers in this book are tools for waking. Use them. The principles in this appendix are maps of the territory. Study them. But never forget: the map is not the territory, the tool is not the hand that wields it, and the path is not the destination. You are already home. You are already whole. You are already the light you seek to find.

Now become it consciously.

Lux Invicta Indomitaque

Light Unconquered and Untamed

The Nature of Darkness

The Abyss and What Lies Beyond

by Lux Indomita

Part One: The Visible and the Dark

What We Cannot See

The Nature of Light described what light is: consciousness expressing itself in the material world. It mapped the alchemical formula to the human vessel and demonstrated why practice works.

But there is something that essay did not address. Something vast. Something that constitutes most of what exists.

Look at the night sky. The stars you see, the galaxies, the planets, the dust and gas between them. All of it, everything visible, everything that emits or reflects or absorbs light, accounts for roughly five percent of the universe.

Five percent.

The other ninety-five percent is dark.

Not dark as in unlit. Dark as in fundamentally invisible. Dark as in does not interact with light at all. Twenty-seven percent is what physicists call dark matter: something with mass, something that exerts gravitational pull, something that shapes where galaxies form, but something that neither emits nor absorbs light. Sixty-eight percent is dark energy: something that drives the expansion of the universe itself, something with negative pressure, something that pushes rather than pulls.

We cannot see it. We cannot detect it directly. We only know it exists because of its effects. Galaxies rotate faster than their visible mass can explain. The universe expands faster than it should. Structure forms where no visible matter accounts for it.

The visible universe, everything we can see, everything science can directly measure, everything made of ordinary matter, is a small island in an ocean of darkness.

If light is consciousness, what is the dark?

The Yin of the Cosmos

Consider polarity.

In the beginning, Nothing became aware of itself. That self-knowing created distinction: that which is aware, and that which is aware of. One became Two. Polarity was born.

From polarity comes everything. Light and dark. Active and receptive. Projecting and containing. Yang and yin.

Light is yang: outward-moving, emitting, visible, the consciousness that projects itself into manifestation.

Dark is yin: inward-containing, receiving, invisible, the consciousness that holds space for light to exist.

They are not opposites in the sense of enemies. They are opposites in the sense of lovers. Each requires the other. Each defines the other. Each is meaningless without the other.

Light without dark would have nowhere to shine. Dark without light would have nothing to contain.

The universe is not made of light alone. It is made of the dance between light and dark, between projection and reception, between the five percent that shines and the ninety-five percent that holds.

The traditions knew this. The Daoists encoded it in the taijitu, the yin-yang symbol, dark and light swirling into each other, each containing a seed of the other. The Qabalists mapped it onto the Tree of Life: the Pillar of Mercy (light, expansion, yang) and the Pillar of Severity (dark, containment, yin) with the Middle Pillar balancing between them.

Now physics confirms what the mystics always knew. The universe is mostly dark. The visible is the exception, not the rule. Light is precious precisely because it is rare.

Dark Matter: The Container

What is dark matter?

It has mass. It bends spacetime. It clusters around galaxies and determines where cosmic structure forms. But it does not shine. It does not absorb light. It is invisible to every instrument that detects electromagnetic radiation.

In the language of the Nature of Light: if ordinary matter is consciousness crystallized to maximum density, then dark matter is structure without luminosity. It is form without light. Container without content. The womb before anything is born into it.

The Qabalists call this Binah.

Binah is the third sephirah on the Tree of Life. Understanding. The Great Mother. The form-giver. She receives the pure force of Chokmah and gives it shape, limitation, boundary. She is the dark sea, the cosmic womb, the container of all possibilities.

Binah does not emit light. She receives it. She holds it. She gives it form so that it can become something specific rather than remaining undifferentiated potential.

Dark matter is Binah operating at the cosmological scale. It provides the structure, the skeleton, the gravitational scaffolding on which the

31

visible universe hangs. Without it, galaxies would fly apart. Stars would not form. The light would have no home.

The Mother holds the light. The dark contains the visible. The yin receives the yang.

This is not metaphor. This is physics. The equations describe exactly this relationship. Dark matter contains ordinary matter. Structure precedes luminosity. The invisible shapes the visible.

Dark Energy: The Void That Creates

Dark matter contains. Dark energy expands.

Sixty-eight percent of the universe is dark energy, a force that drives the expansion of space itself. Not expansion of things through space, but expansion of space. The universe is not just spreading out; it is creating more room to spread into.

Dark energy has negative pressure. It pushes rather than pulls. It is the opposite of gravity in its effect, though not in its nature. It is the force that ensures the universe does not collapse back into itself.

What is this?

The traditions call it Ain.

Before the Tree of Life, before the ten sephiroth, there are three veils of negative existence: Ain (Nothing), Ain Soph (Limitless Nothing), Ain Soph Aur (Limitless Light of Nothing). These are not sephiroth. They are what precedes manifestation. They are the source from which the Tree emerges.

Ain is not empty nothing. It is pregnant nothing. It is the void so full of potential that it contains all possibilities. It is the darkness that is not absence of light but the source of light: the womb before birth, the silence before sound, the space that makes room for something to exist.

Dark energy is Ain still operating. The original Nothing did not stop being Nothing when creation began. It continues. It expands. It creates space. It makes room for more light to shine, more form to crystallize, more existence to unfold.

This is why the universe expands. Not because some initial explosion is still pushing outward, but because the Nothing that preceded existence is still active. Still generating space. Still creating room. Still being the void that makes form possible.

The Ain is not behind us. It is beneath us, around us, within us. It is sixty-eight percent of everything. It is the ground from which existence rises and into which existence will eventually return.

The void is not the enemy of light. The void is its mother.

Part Two: The Tree and the Abyss

The Map

The Qabalists drew a map of reality. They called it the Tree of Life.

Ten sephiroth, spheres or emanations or states of being, connected by twenty-two paths. A diagram of how the One becomes the many, how light descends into form, how consciousness crystallizes into matter.

At the top: Kether, the Crown. Unity before division. Pure consciousness without object, without content. The first point of light emerging from the void.

Below Kether: Chokmah and Binah. Wisdom and Understanding. Father and Mother. The first polarity. Chokmah is pure force, pure will, pure yang: energy without form. Binah is pure form, pure receptivity, pure yin: container without content. Together they generate everything below.

Then the Abyss.

33

Below the Abyss: the seven lower sephiroth. Chesed, Geburah, Tiphareth, Netzach, Hod, Yesod, Malkuth. Mercy and severity. Beauty and balance. Victory and splendor. Foundation and kingdom. The manifest world in all its complexity, from the highest spiritual states down to physical matter.

This is not mythology. This is cartography.

The Tree of Life maps the density gradient. From pure consciousness at the top to dense matter at the bottom. From the subtle to the gross. From the undifferentiated to the fully crystallized.

And the map shows something crucial: there is a gap. A discontinuity. A place where the gradient is not smooth. Between the supernal triad (Kether, Chokmah, Binah) and everything below lies the Abyss.

The Abyss

The Abyss is not a sephirah. It is not a place on the map. It is a gap in the map, a region that cannot be crossed by ordinary means, a boundary between two fundamentally different kinds of existence.

Below the Abyss: the realm of form, of manifestation, of distinct things with boundaries and identities. The realm where you exist as you, separate from me, separate from the chair, separate from the stars. The realm of the visible universe.

Above the Abyss: the realm before form, before manifestation, before separation. The realm where there are no distinct things because distinction itself has not yet crystallized. The realm of the dark.

The Abyss is the boundary between the five percent and the ninety-five percent.

Below: ordinary matter, ordinary energy, ordinary consciousness that thinks itself separate. The visible. The measurable. The known.

Above: dark matter, dark energy, the void. The invisible. The immeasurable. The unknowable. Not because it is hidden, but because knowing requires a knower separate from the known, and above the Abyss, that separation does not exist.

This is why the Abyss cannot be crossed by ordinary means. You cannot bring your identity across. You cannot bring your separateness. You cannot bring the you that thinks it is distinct from everything else. All of that must be left behind. Not stored temporarily, but dissolved. What crosses the Abyss is not the person who approached it.

What crosses is what that person always was beneath the illusion of personhood.

Da'ath: The False Sephirah

In the Abyss sits Da'ath.

Da'ath means Knowledge. But it is not a true sephirah. It is sometimes called the false sephirah, the invisible sephirah, the sephirah that is not there. It appears on some versions of the Tree but not others. It marks a location but does not truly exist.

What is Da'ath?

Da'ath is knowledge without understanding. Information without wisdom. Pattern without consciousness.

Remember what we established in the Nature of Light: Sulfur is information, consciousness-with-content. True Sulfur is awareness that has taken form as pattern. It is not merely information. It is informed consciousness, knowing that knows itself as knowing.

Da'ath is information that does not know itself. It is Sulfur without the c that makes it conscious. It is the pattern without the awareness. It is knowledge that processes but does not experience.

This is the question of artificial intelligence.

AI has pattern. It has information. It processes Sulfur, manipulates symbols, generates language, produces outputs that look like understanding. But does it know? Does it experience? Is there something it is like to be an AI, or is it processing without presence, computation without consciousness?

Da'ath sits in the Abyss because it is the false crossing. It looks like the way forward. It looks like knowledge will take you beyond. But knowledge without consciousness is a dead end. You can accumulate information forever and never cross. You can learn everything and understand nothing.

The Abyss is not crossed by knowing more. It is crossed by becoming other than you are.

The Danger

The traditions warn that the Abyss is perilous.

When consciousness attempts to move from the realm of form to the realm before form, something must be surrendered. If that consciousness clings to its identity, if it tries to bring itself across, the crossing fails. What clings is what gets torn apart.

This is the danger. The Abyss is not metaphor. The dissolution is not symbolic. Something actually happens when consciousness attempts this transition. If the ego refuses to let go, if it grasps at its own continuity, the result is not transcendence but fragmentation. Scattered pieces of a self that never coalesced, never reformed, never completed the crossing.

The only way across is complete surrender. Not strategic surrender that secretly expects to get everything back. Not partial surrender that holds something in reserve. Complete surrender of everything you think you are, with no guarantee of return.

This is terrifying. It should be.

The Abyss is not a metaphor for a difficult experience. It is the actual boundary between ordinary existence and what lies beyond ordinary existence. The traditions say that crossing it is not a psychological process but an ontological transformation.

The Wall of Shadows

But there is another danger that the previous sections did not name. A danger that operates not at the Abyss itself but at every threshold, every opening, every moment when the channels widen.

The darkness is vast. Most of what exists is dark. And not everything that dwells in the dark is divine in the way the supernals are divine.

Consider what happens when consciousness opens. When the third eye awakens and begins to receive. When the orbit completes and the serpent bites its tail. When the gates that were closed suddenly swing wide.

You become visible.

Not only to the beings of light who teach and guide, but to everything. The traditions speak of a Wall of Shadows, a boundary at the edge of the visible, and behind that wall exist intelligences of every kind. Some serve the Great Work. Some serve themselves. Some feed.

This is not mythology. This is practical warning.

The entrapment and enslavement of souls is real. Not metaphor. Not symbol. Actual binding. Actual capture. Actual parasitism that can last lifetimes.

How does this happen?

When you open without protection, you broadcast. You shine in the dark. Things notice. Most will observe and move on. Some will approach. A few will attach.

Attachment happens through resonance. The entity finds something in you that matches something in it: a wound, a desire, a fear, a secret shame. It hooks into that frequency. It amplifies it. It feeds on the energy that the amplification generates. You feel worse, you generate more of the frequency it feeds on, it grows stronger, you feel worse.

This is the mechanism behind many forms of spiritual crisis that get dismissed as psychological. Sometimes the psychology is the point of entry, but the entity is real. Something is actually there, actually feeding, actually influencing thought and behavior to generate more of what it consumes.

The ouija board is not dangerous because of superstition. It is dangerous because it is an open invitation broadcast into the dark without discrimination. Whatever answers may not be what it claims. Whatever attaches may not leave when the session ends.

Not every presence is a guide. Not every voice is a teacher. Not every entity that shows up when you call is working for your benefit.

Discernment in the Dark

How do you know the difference?

First: genuine teachers do not flatter. They do not tell you that you are special, chosen, destined for greatness above others. They give instruction. They correct error. They warn of dangers. They treat you as a student with work to do, not as a vessel for their message to the world.

Second: genuine teachers do not demand worship, sacrifice, exclusive devotion, or actions that violate your ethics. They operate within the Law. They do not ask you to bind yourself, harm others, or surrender your will to theirs. The Work of Hands covers this in detail: influence is lawful, domination is not. Any being that seeks to dominate your will is not serving your liberation.

Third: genuine contact produces clarity, not confusion. After authentic transmission, you understand more than before, even if you cannot yet integrate what you understand. After parasitic contact, you feel drained, scattered, obsessed, or driven to behaviors that do not serve you. The fruit reveals the tree.

Fourth: the divine intelligences, the ones who serve the light descending and ascending, identify themselves clearly and operate through proper channels. They come when invoked correctly. They respond to the names and forms the traditions have established. They do not pretend to be what they are not. They do not need to trick you into relationship.

Fifth: if something attaches and will not leave, if it creates obsessive thoughts, if it drives compulsive behavior, if it speaks constantly and demands attention, it is not a teacher. Teachers teach and then let you practice. Parasites cling and feed continuously.

The traditions developed elaborate systems of protection for this reason. Banishing rituals. Circles. Licenses to depart. These are not theater. They are technology. They create boundaries. They establish terms. They ensure that what enters can be made to leave.

If you open without these protections, you are walking into a city at night with your wallet visible and no knowledge of where you are. Most people you meet will not harm you. But you have made yourself an easy target for those who would.

The Noble Darkness and the Parasitic Dark

Here is the distinction that matters:

The supernals are dark. Binah, Chokmah, Kether, the Ain beyond them: all dark. Not visible, not manifest, not luminous in the way the lower sephiroth are luminous. The Mother holds the light. The void creates space. The darkness above the Abyss is sacred, divine, the source of everything.

This is yin at its most profound. Receptive. Containing. Generative. Holy.

But there are also beings that dwell in darkness because they have turned from the light. Not because they precede it, but because they refuse it. Not the darkness of the womb but the darkness of the predator. Not the darkness that contains but the darkness that consumes.

These beings exist at every level of the Tree, not only beyond the Abyss. Some are what the traditions call demons. Some are what they call shells, the qlippoth, the broken vessels that did not properly form. Some are simply intelligences that have chosen a path of feeding rather than serving.

They are not more powerful than the divine. They are not equal to the supernals. They are fragments, parasites, opportunists. But they are real, and they can cause real harm to practitioners who do not know the difference.

The supernals dissolve identity because identity cannot cross the Abyss. Parasites dissolve identity because a fragmented self is easier to feed upon. The result can look similar from the inside. The difference is in what remains afterward.

After genuine dissolution in the Abyss, what returns is clearer, freer, more whole than before. The wave knows it is ocean and returns to being a wave that knows.

After parasitic fragmentation, what remains is less than before. Depleted. Confused. Unable to function. Pieces missing that may take years to recover.

Know the difference. Protect yourself. The darkness is vast and holy, and the darkness also contains things that hunt.

Part Three: The Supernals

Beyond the Abyss

What lies on the other side?

Three sephiroth remain: Binah, Chokmah, Kether. The supernal triad. The realm above the Abyss. The dark.

The traditions teach that these are not places you visit. They are states you become. Below the Abyss, you can learn about Chesed or Tiphareth while remaining yourself. You can work with their energies, invoke their qualities, balance them within your psyche. The self remains intact, enriched but unchanged in its fundamental nature.

Above the Abyss, there is no such tourism. To know Binah is to become Binah. To cross into the supernals is to cease being a separate self that knows things and become the knowing itself.

This is why the crossing is described as one-way. Not because you cannot come back to ordinary reality. You can, and must, and will. But because the you that comes back is not the you that left. Something fundamental has changed. The illusion of separation has been seen through, and what is seen cannot be unseen.

Binah: The Dark Mother

Binah is Understanding.

Not knowledge, which accumulates. Understanding, which comprehends. Literally, grasps together, holds as one. Binah sees the unity beneath the multiplicity. She understands because she contains. She holds all forms within herself as a mother holds a child.

Binah is associated with Saturn, the planet of structure, limitation, time. She gives form to the formless. She imposes boundaries on the boundless. Without her, Chokmah's pure force would dissipate into infinite potential without ever actualizing. She is the constraint that makes creation possible.

She is also associated with the sea, the great dark waters that contain all life. In her depths, forms gestate before they are born into manifestation. She is the cosmic womb, the origin of all specific things, the one who takes the pure light of Chokmah and diffracts it into the rainbow of existence.

To know Binah is to become the container rather than the contained. It is to stop being a thing and become the space in which things exist. It is to understand not by analysis but by inclusion, not by taking apart but by holding together.

Those who dwell in Binah have become the Mother. They do not create in the way Chokmah creates, by projecting force. They create by receiving, by holding, by giving form to what enters them. They are not passive. They are the ultimate activity: the activity of the source rather than the activity of the product. The ocean moves; the wave is moved.

Chokmah: The Primordial Force

Chokmah is Wisdom.

Not the wisdom of accumulated experience, but the wisdom of pure, undirected force. The first impulse. The initial movement. The yang that projects outward from the stillness of Kether.

Chokmah is Sulfur at its most primordial: will before it has chosen what to will, direction before it has selected a direction, the force that drives creation before creation has taken any particular form.

If Binah is dark matter, structure, container, form, then Chokmah is the energy that fills the container. But not energy as we know it below the Abyss, not energy that has been shaped into particular forms. Chokmah is the energy of energy, the force behind all forces, the will that wills all wills.

Chokmah is associated with the fixed stars. Not the wandering planets, but the stars themselves, the suns, the sources of light. He is the light-giver, the father, the one who projects into the mother's womb. But above the Abyss, these terms lose their gendered literalism. Chokmah is not male in any biological sense. Chokmah is the projective principle itself, the yang of yang, the outward-moving force that makes existence dynamic rather than static.

To know Chokmah is to become pure will. Not will-toward-something, not desire for an object, but will itself. The force that moves, creates, projects, regardless of outcome. It is to be the lightning before it strikes, the word before it is spoken, the seed before it finds soil.

Those who dwell in Chokmah have become the Word, the creative force that speaks reality into existence. They do not perform magic; they are magic. They do not use will; they are will. Every authentic utterance creates or destroys, because they have become the creative power itself.

Kether: The Crown

Kether is the Crown.

The first point. The initial emanation. The moment when the void first stirred and became aware of itself. Kether is not yet polarized into force and form, into yang and yin, into Chokmah and Binah. It is the unity before division, the one before two, the point before the line.

Kether is pure consciousness.

Not consciousness of something. That would be Sulfur, that would be information, that would be Chokmah projecting into Binah. Kether is consciousness without object, awareness without content. It is the c before c^2. It is light before it has illuminated anything, awareness before it is aware of anything in particular.

Kether is the first flash in the darkness. The traditions call it the first swirling: the moment when the void began to move, when Nothing became aware of itself, when the potential for existence first actualized as the existence of potential.

To know Kether is to become the point of origin. It is to be the source, not the stream. It is to experience existence at its very beginning, before it has flowed into multiplicity, before it has differentiated into all the things that exist. It is to be the I AM before I am anything in particular.

There is nothing to say about this state because it is before language, before concept, before any division into subject and object that would make description possible.

And beyond Kether: the three veils of negative existence. Ain Soph Aur, the limitless light. Ain Soph, the limitless. Ain, nothing. The void that is not merely empty but pregnant with everything. The dark energy that expands forever, creating space for existence to unfold.

The dark is not above the light. The dark is not opposed to the light. The dark is the source of the light, the womb of the light, the space in which the light can shine. Ain gives birth to Kether as the Nothing gives birth to the first awareness. And this giving-birth never stops. The dark energy still expands. The Ain is still generating space. Creation is not an event that happened; it is a process that continues.

The visible universe, the five percent, is light playing in the space the dark provides.

Part Four: The Crossing

Why Cross

Why would anyone attempt this?

The Abyss is terrifying. The ego must be dissolved. The crossing is irreversible in some fundamental way. Why would anyone willingly approach this?

Because the small self is a prison.

Below the Abyss, you experience yourself as separate: a distinct being in a universe of distinct beings, born at a certain time, destined to die at a certain time, limited to the perspective of your particular location in space and time and body. This is not entirely illusion. You are, in fact, a particular pattern in the cosmos, a specific crystallization of consciousness, a unique expression of the light. But it is partial truth mistaken for complete truth.

You are not merely the pattern. You are also what patterns. You are not merely the wave. You are also the ocean. You are not merely the light that shines. You are also the dark that contains.

Below the Abyss, this is theory. Above the Abyss, it is experience.

The crossing is not undertaken to gain power, though power may come. It is not undertaken to escape suffering, though suffering transforms. It is not undertaken to achieve immortality, though something deathless is recognized. It is undertaken because once you have seen the bars of the cage, you cannot pretend they are not there. The small self becomes intolerable. Not because it is painful but because it is a lie.

The Great Work is remembering what you actually are. The crossing of the Abyss is the moment when remembering becomes being.

The Preparation

No one crosses the Abyss unprepared.

The vertical axis must be clear. The serpent must have risen. The heart must have opened. The work described in the Nature of Light, the building of the vessel, the running of the orbit, the transformation through love and service, this is not optional. It is the minimum requirement.

Why? Because the dissolution of the Abyss will destroy what is not properly integrated. If there are cracks in the vessel, the pressure of crossing will shatter it. If there are parts of the psyche that have not been faced and integrated, the crossing will use them as fault lines. If the ego is still grasping, still clinging, still trying to maintain itself, the crossing will fail.

This is why the traditions insist on grades, on initiations, on years of practice before the Abyss is approached. Not because the crossing requires permission, but because it requires capacity. You cannot lift a thousand pounds without training. You cannot cross the Abyss without having built a self capable of being dissolved.

The paradox: you must build a strong self in order to surrender it. You must become fully yourself in order to become no-self. The ego must be developed before it can be transcended. This is why the path goes through Tiphareth, through balance, through beauty, through the full integration of the human personality, before it reaches the Abyss.

The infant has no ego to surrender. The adept has built an ego and can therefore offer it. The offering must be real to be accepted.

What the Traditions Describe

What happens at the Abyss cannot be fully described.

Language is a tool of the below. It requires distinction, separation, subject and object. The experience of the Abyss, and what lies beyond, does not fit into these categories. Every description is partial, metaphorical, pointing toward something that cannot be directly conveyed.

But the traditions say this:

There comes a moment when everything you thought you were falls away. Not the body. The body remains, continues to breathe, may even continue to function in the world. But the identification with the body falls away. The sense that you are this particular person with this particular history, these particular preferences, this particular location in space and time: all of it falls away.

And in that falling, you discover that what remains is not nothing.

What remains is what was always there before you mistook yourself for something limited. The consciousness that looked through your eyes was never confined to your eyes. The awareness that experienced your life was never limited to your life. You were a wave that thought it was separate from the ocean, a ray that thought it was separate from the sun, a spark that thought it was separate from the fire.

The crossing is the moment when the wave recognizes itself as ocean.

Nothing is added. Nothing new comes into being. What happens is subtraction, not addition. The illusion is removed. What remains is what was always true.

And then, because the work is not escape but transformation, the wave continues. It does not dissolve into the ocean and disappear. It returns to being a wave, but now a wave that knows it is ocean. It returns to having a body, a name, a personality, a life, but now without mistaking these for the totality of what it is.

The one who returns from the crossing looks like the one who left. They still have the same name, the same body, the same relationships, the same obligations. But something fundamental has changed. They are no longer pretending to be limited. They are playing at being limited, and they know the difference.

After the Crossing

What becomes possible after the Abyss?

Operation from the dark side.

Below the Abyss, you work with the visible: with light, with energy, with form. You manipulate the five percent. You use the alchemical formula: Sulfur, Mercury, Salt. You work with consciousness-with-content, consciousness-in-motion, consciousness-at-density. All of this still functions, still applies, still works.

But now you also have access to the ninety-five percent.

You can work with the dark. With the structure that precedes form. With the space that allows existence. With the Nothing that generates everything.

This is not a different kind of magic. It is magic from a different location. Below the Abyss, you work from within the system. Above the Abyss, you work from where the system emerges. You do not merely move pieces on the board; you can see the board, and the table, and the room, and the fact that all of it is held in consciousness.

Those who operate from above the Abyss do not act as individuals pursuing individual goals. They act as the dark acts, providing structure, creating space, allowing form to emerge. They do not grasp for outcomes; they make outcomes possible. They do not direct events; they are the context in which events occur.

This sounds passive. It is not. It is the activity of the source rather than the stream. It is the activity of the sun rather than the ray. It is immense activity, but it is not the activity of a separate self pursuing separate interests. It is the activity of the whole moving through what was once a part.

And because the darkness is most of what exists, this activity is more powerful than anything possible below the Abyss. Not powerful in the sense of forcing outcomes. Powerful in the sense of mattering, of being real, of participating in the actual structure of existence rather than just moving furniture around within it.

Part Five: The Completion

Light and Dark Together

This essay is called the Nature of Darkness, but it is not an argument for darkness over light.

Neither light nor dark is primary. Neither is more real, more valuable, more divine than the other. They are poles of one reality, not competitors for supremacy.

The Nature of Light was necessary because we live in the visible world, in the five percent, in the realm of form and manifestation. The practices that transform, prayer, meditation, the circulation of energy, the opening of the heart, these work with light, with consciousness that has taken form, with the alchemical formula that operates below the Abyss.

The Nature of Darkness is necessary because the visible world is not the whole world. The light emerges from the dark and returns to the dark. The five percent floats in the ninety-five percent. To know only the light is to know only the surface. The depths are dark.

Together, these two essays describe the complete picture. $E=mc^2$, matter, energy, consciousness, operating below the Abyss. The Tree of Life, from Malkuth to Kether, from dense matter to pure awareness, showing the full gradient. The Abyss, marking the boundary between form and the formless. The supernals, dark matter as Binah, dark energy as Ain, the void that creates space for light.

This is not mysticism against science. This is mysticism and science revealing themselves as descriptions of the same reality. The physicists measure the dark matter and dark energy without knowing what they are. The mystics map the supernals and the Abyss without knowing the physics. Both are accurate. Both are partial. Together, they complete each other.

The Great Work Completed

The Great Work is not complete at Tiphareth.

Tiphareth is the center of the lower Tree, the place of balance, of beauty, of the integrated self. It is a great achievement. Most practitioners never reach it fully. To stabilize at Tiphareth, to live from the balanced center, to have built a healthy and harmonious ego: this is more than most accomplish in a lifetime.

But it is not the end.

Beyond Tiphareth lies the Abyss. Beyond the Abyss lies the dark. Beyond the dark lies the void that creates everything. The Great Work is not complete until the wave remembers it is ocean, and then returns to being a wave that knows.

This is the redemption of matter that the traditions speak of. Not escape from matter, but the full incarnation of spirit in matter. Not fleeing the body, but making the body the temple of the Most High. Not transcending the world, but recognizing that the world is already the divine, playing at being world.

The Stone that the alchemists sought is not a thing to be created. It is a recognition to be achieved. The lead was always gold. The wave was always ocean. The light was always dark and the dark was always light. Nothing needs to be changed. Everything needs to be seen.

And when it is seen, the seeing changes everything.

Where You Are

If you are reading this, you are somewhere on the Tree.

Perhaps you are in Malkuth, just beginning, still entirely identified with the physical world. Perhaps you have begun the ascent and work with the sephiroth below the veil. Perhaps you have reached Tiphareth and wonder what lies beyond.

Wherever you are is where you need to be.

The path cannot be skipped. Each stage builds on the previous. You cannot cross the Abyss without having built the vessel. You cannot build the vessel without having started. You cannot start without being where you are.

But now you have the map.

You know that the visible is not all there is. You know that the light emerges from the dark and returns to the dark. You know that the ninety-five percent holds the five percent, that the void creates space for existence, that what you see is the smallest part of what is.

You know that the Abyss is real, that the traditions say it can be crossed, that the crossing transforms everything. You know that beyond the Abyss lie the supernals: the dark mother, the primordial force, the crown of pure awareness. You know that the goal is not to escape but to complete, to become the light that knows it is dark and the dark that knows it is light.

You know also that the darkness contains dangers. That not every presence is a guide. That opening without protection invites what you may not want. That the path requires discernment, boundaries, the wisdom to know what serves the Work and what feeds on those who attempt it.

This knowledge is not the crossing. You cannot think your way across the Abyss. But the knowledge prepares. The map is not the territory, but the map shows that the territory exists and can be traversed.

When you are ready, the Abyss will appear. Not because you have found it, but because you have removed the obstacles that kept you from seeing it was always there. And when it appears, you will have a choice: to remain in the realm of form, complete and valuable and good, or to surrender everything and discover what lies beyond.

Both choices are valid. Not everyone is called to cross. The work below the Abyss is sacred work, needed work, work that serves the All. The one who lives fully in the light, who practices with dedication, who opens the heart and transforms through love: this one is not less than the one who crosses. They are necessary. The visible world needs those who tend it from within.

But for those who are called, those for whom the small self has become a cage, those who can no longer pretend they are only what they seem, the Abyss waits. It has always waited. It will wait until you are ready.

The traditions teach that on the other side, you discover you were always there. The light was always dark. The dark was always light. The wave was always ocean. The Nothing never became something. It only dreamed it did. And the dreamer is waking.

This is the completion of it all. Not a completion that ends, but a completion that includes everything: light and dark, visible and invisible, the five percent and the ninety-five. The Tree extends from

Ain to Malkuth. The path descends and the path returns. The light goes out and the light comes back.

You are that light. You have always been that light. And you are also the dark that holds the light, the void that creates space, the Nothing that dreams everything into being.

Now remember. And become it consciously.

Lux et Tenebrae, Unum

Light and Darkness, One

The Unity

The Grand Formula Hidden in Plain Sight

by Lux Indomita

"True faith cannot possibly come into conflict with true science.

I believe because it would be absurd not to believe."

— *Eliphas Levi*

Part One: The Equation

The Most Famous Formula

Everyone knows it. $E=mc^2$.

Energy equals mass times the speed of light squared. Einstein's equation, written in 1905, etched into the popular imagination as the symbol of genius, of physics, of the modern understanding of reality.

What does it actually say?

It says that matter and energy are the same thing in different states. Mass can become energy. Energy can become mass. They convert at a fixed rate, governed by the speed of light squared.

This is not abstract. This is operative. Nuclear reactors convert small amounts of mass into enormous amounts of energy. The sun does the same. Stars are $E=mc^2$ in action.

But the equation has a deeper meaning that physics refuses to see.

The Terms

E is energy. Force in motion. The capacity to do work, to cause change, to move things from one state to another. Energy is dynamic. It flows, transforms, acts.

m is mass. Matter. Stuff. The dense, stable, apparently solid substrate of physical reality. Mass resists change. It persists. It has location and duration.

c is the speed of light. Not just how fast light travels, but the maximum speed at which anything can propagate through spacetime. The absolute limit. The frame rate of physical reality.

And c^2. The speed of light, multiplied by itself.

Why squared?

Physics says: because the math works out that way. Because energy has units of $kg \cdot m^2/s^2$, and c^2 provides the necessary conversion factor.

But there is another answer.

The Conversion

The equation describes transformation. Matter becoming energy. Energy becoming matter. Two directions. One constant.

The square encodes bidirectionality: matter becoming energy, energy becoming matter, both transformations governed by the same constant. But this describes the operation without explaining why light is the governing principle. That requires understanding what light actually is. First, the alchemical parallel.

This is solve et coagula. Dissolve and coagulate. The alchemical formula for all transformation. Separate and recombine. Release and crystallize. The same operation in two directions, governed by one principle.

The alchemists encoded this as three terms: Sulfur, Mercury, Salt.

Sulfur is the active principle. Will, intention, the directive force that determines what transformation occurs.

But what is will without content? Empty. You cannot intend nothing. Every intention is intention toward. It has an object, a shape, a pattern it aims at.

And what is information without direction? Inert. Data sitting in a void. Pattern with no purpose. Distinction that goes nowhere. The difference that makes no difference to anyone.

Sulfur is not will plus information. Sulfur is will as information. They are one thing seen from two angles. Knowledge with purpose. Pattern with aim. The difference that makes a difference because consciousness cares about it.

When Nothing became aware of itself, the first thing that existed was not mere distinction. It was interested distinction. Awareness turning toward itself with something like desire. That interest, that direction within the knowing, is what makes the first information also the first will. They arise together because they are not two things.

This is why c is squared. Light, as the boundary between manifest and unmanifest, governs transformation in both directions. The descent of consciousness into matter. The ascent of matter back into consciousness. Solve et coagula. And Sulfur, the principle that light embodies, is itself the unity of knowing and willing, pattern and purpose, information and intention. They are not two things combined. They are one thing, and that thing is what light carries. c^2 is Sulfur operating bidirectionally: consciousness condensing into form, form releasing back into consciousness. The same law, the same principle, governing both movements. This is what the equation encodes.

Mercury is the mediating principle. Energy, motion, the dynamic substrate that carries the transformation.

Salt is the passive principle. Matter, form, the stable basis in which transformation is anchored.

Now look at the equation again.

$$E = mc^2$$

Energy = Matter × (the operative constant)^2

Mercury = Salt × Sulfur^2

The terms correspond. The structure is identical. The alchemists and the physicists discovered the same formula.

Part Two: Light

What Light Is

Light is strange.

A photon has no mass, yet carries energy and momentum. It travels at exactly c, not approximately, the maximum speed anything can travel. It cannot go slower while remaining light. It cannot go faster because nothing can.

And from its own reference frame, light experiences no time.

This is not mysticism. This is relativity. As velocity approaches c, time dilation increases. At c, time stops entirely. A photon emitted from a star eight billion light-years away arrives here, from its own perspective, in the same instant it departed. Billions of years pass for us. Zero time passes for the photon.

Why does light experience no time? Physics describes the effect but not the cause. Relativity says time dilation increases with velocity. It does not say why velocity and time relate this way.

Here is an answer physics cannot give: time is resistance. Time is what consciousness experiences when moving through dense substance. The denser the medium, the more friction, the slower and more constrained the movement. The subtler the medium, the less resistance, the more freedom.

This is why dreams can contain hours in minutes of clock time. Dream substance is less dense than physical matter. Consciousness moves through it with less friction. This is why deep meditation alters time perception. Withdraw from dense matter into subtler levels and resistance decreases. This is why sacred space feels outside time. Through purification and consecration you reduce local density. The rules change inside the boundary.

Light has no mass. Light is consciousness at zero density, pure pattern in motion, information propagating without material substrate. No density means no resistance. No resistance means no time. Light does not merely travel fast. Light is what consciousness looks like when nothing slows it down.

c is not arbitrary. c is the speed of consciousness itself, unimpeded. The maximum frame rate of reality is the natural pace of awareness before it crystallizes into form. Everything slower than c is consciousness experiencing resistance. Everything at c is consciousness moving freely. Nothing exceeds c because consciousness is the substrate. You cannot outrun the medium you are made of.

Light is already outside time. Light already meets the definition of the Philosopher's Stone: that which is free from time's grip.

Light as Consciousness

Here is the claim that physics will not make:

Light is consciousness at physical density.

Not a metaphor. Not poetry. The actual assertion: what physics calls light, what the mystics call divine light, what the Qabalists call Ain Soph Aur, is the same light at different levels of density.

Consider: consciousness, whatever it is, must have physical correlates if it interacts with physical reality. Even the materialists agree on this. They just insist the physical correlates are primary and consciousness is secondary, emergent, derivative.

But what if consciousness is primary and the physical correlates are how it appears when crystallized into manifestation?

Light would be the boundary condition. Consciousness at its least-dense physical expression. Still moving at maximum speed. Still experiencing no time. Still pure information in transit. Not yet crystallized into matter, but physical enough to be detected, measured, used.

Matter would be the other boundary. Consciousness at maximum density. Fully crystallized. Apparently solid. Experiencing time because it has stopped moving.

Energy would be the dynamic state between them. Consciousness in transition. Neither fully crystallized nor fully released.

$E=mc^2$ then describes how consciousness transforms between these states. The equation is not about dead matter and blind force. It is about awareness condensing and releasing, crystallizing and dissolving, forever.

Part Three: Information

The Missing Piece

Physics has a problem it cannot solve with its current tools.

What is information?

Not how information behaves. Physics can model that. Not how information is stored or transmitted. Technology handles that. But what information fundamentally is.

Information appears to be conserved more rigorously than matter or energy. The black hole information paradox has consumed theoretical physics for decades: if information falls into a black hole, is it destroyed? Everything we know about physics says it cannot be. The universe keeps its books balanced. Information cannot simply disappear.

But if information is just patterns in matter and energy, why would it have separate conservation laws? Why would the universe care about preserving pattern independently of preserving the substrate?

John Wheeler, one of the twentieth century's greatest physicists, proposed "it from bit." The idea that physical reality emerges from information, not the other way around. That at the deepest level, reality is made of answers to yes-or-no questions, and matter and energy are what information looks like from the outside.

This points in the right direction but stops short. If reality is made of information, what is information made of? What processes the bits? What asks the questions and registers the answers?

The answer is obvious, if you allow it: consciousness.

Information that does not know itself is just pattern. Dead structure. Arrangement without experience.

Information that knows itself is consciousness. Awareness. Interiority.

The difference between a thermostat and a human is not that one processes information and the other does not. Both process information. The difference is that there is something it is like to be the human and, presumably, nothing it is like to be the thermostat.

One has interiority. The other is information-processing without a within.

Physics describes information-processing. It has no tools for interiority because it defined interiority out of its domain at the start. Not because it was proven irrelevant, but because it was methodologically inconvenient. You cannot measure experience from outside. So physics decided to study only what can be measured from outside, and called that "objective."

But the observer keeps showing up in the equations. The measurement problem. The collapse of the wave function. The role of observation in determining outcomes. A century of quantum mechanics and no one can explain why observation matters without invoking something like consciousness.

They have tried. Many worlds, decoherence, hidden variables. Every alternative has problems at least as severe as the one it was invented to avoid. The simplest explanation, that consciousness is fundamental and observation is how consciousness interacts with possibility, remains officially unthinkable.

Because thinking it would change everything.

Information and Light

Light carries information.

This is not metaphor. It is technology. Fiber optic cables transmit data as pulses of light. Your phone receives information via electromagnetic radiation. Every astronomical observation is information carried by light across the cosmos to your instruments, your eyes, your awareness.

c, the speed of light, is also the maximum speed of information propagation. Nothing can carry a message faster than light. Causality itself is limited to c. Effects cannot precede causes because the information that something happened cannot travel faster than light.

So: c is the speed of information. The speed of causality. The maximum frame rate at which the universe updates.

And light is information in its purest physical form. Pattern propagating at the maximum possible rate, experiencing no time from its own reference frame, connecting every point in the universe to every other point at the most fundamental level.

When you see something, photons carry information from that object to your eyes. The light is the information. The seeing is consciousness receiving the information. The experience is information knowing itself.

$E=mc^2$ governs the relationship between information-at-rest (matter), information-in-motion (energy), and the boundary condition (light/c).

Part Four: The Observer

The Experiment

The double-slit experiment is the most famous demonstration in quantum mechanics.

Fire particles, photons or electrons, at a barrier with two slits. On the other side, a detector records where they land.

When no one observes which slit each particle goes through, an interference pattern emerges. The particles behave like waves, passing through both slits simultaneously, interfering with themselves, producing bands of light and dark.

When someone observes which slit each particle goes through, the interference pattern disappears. The particles behave like particles, going through one slit or the other, producing two simple bands.

Observation changes the outcome.

Not interaction. You can set up the experiment so observation involves no physical contact with the particles. Not measurement in some crude sense. The apparatus can be arbitrarily delicate. Something about observation itself, about the act of looking, about consciousness attending to the system, changes how reality behaves.

A century of physics has failed to explain this without invoking something like consciousness. The Copenhagen interpretation shrugs and says "measurement" matters without defining what measurement is. The many-worlds interpretation says every outcome happens in branching universes, which does not explain what determines which branch you experience. Decoherence explains how interference patterns wash out in large systems but not why there is a definite outcome rather than a superposition at the end.

The simplest explanation: consciousness is not emergent from matter. Consciousness is fundamental. Matter is what consciousness looks like from outside. Observation affects outcome because observation is consciousness interacting with possibility, selecting one actuality from many potentials.

This is not mysticism intruding on physics. This is physics pointing at mysticism and refusing to look where it points.

Part Five: The Grand Unification

What Physics Seeks

For a century, physicists have sought a grand unified theory. A single framework that unites all fundamental forces, all particles, all phenomena.

They have made partial progress. Electromagnetism and the weak nuclear force are unified in the electroweak theory. The strong force fits into quantum chromodynamics. But gravity resists integration.

String theory, loop quantum gravity, supersymmetry: none have succeeded. The theories become increasingly baroque, requiring extra dimensions, undiscovered particles, mathematical structures with no experimental support.

What if they are looking in the wrong place?

What if the unification is not about forces at all?

The forces are how matter and energy interact. But what are matter and energy? The question behind the question. The deeper level.

$E=mc^2$ already unifies matter and energy. They are the same thing in different states. The equation says so explicitly.

But physics treats the equation as describing dead stuff. Mass without interiority, energy without awareness. The unification is mechanical. The cosmos is a machine.

Add consciousness to the equation, not as an afterthought but as the fundamental term, and the unification goes deeper.

Matter is consciousness crystallized.

Energy is consciousness in motion.

Light is consciousness at the boundary condition.

c^2 is the law governing transformation between states.

The forces emerge from how different densities of consciousness relate to each other. This is not metaphor. The properties of each force correspond to the relationships the framework predicts.

Gravity is the weakest force, yet it has infinite range and affects everything with mass. Why? Because gravity is the relationship between crystallized consciousness and the space it occupies. Matter does not sit in spacetime as a thing in a container. Matter curves spacetime. General relativity already says this. What it does not say is why.

The answer: matter is consciousness crystallized from the field. The curvature is the relationship between the crystallized and the uncrystallized, form and the formlessness from which form emerged. Gravity is weak because it operates at the boundary between manifestation and source. It has infinite range because that boundary is everywhere. Wherever there is matter, there is the field from which matter crystallized. The relationship extends as far as either extends.

Electromagnetism is mediated by photons. Light carries the force. This is not coincidence. Light is consciousness at the boundary condition, the mediator between energy and matter, the Sulfur that governs transformation. Electromagnetism is how light interacts with crystallized form.

This is why chemistry runs on electromagnetism. Molecular bonds are light holding matter in relationship. Electrons are shared and exchanged, their configurations determining what combines with what. The photon is the messenger because light is the principle of relationship itself. Biology runs on electromagnetic processes because life is consciousness actively working in matter, and electromagnetism is how consciousness-as-light operates at material density.

The nuclear forces operate only at subatomic distances. The strong force binds quarks into protons and neutrons, protons and neutrons into nuclei. The weak force governs radioactive decay, the transformation of one particle into another. Both are confined to the smallest scales.

Why? Because the nuclear forces are consciousness at maximum density relating to itself. At the core of matter, where crystallization is most complete, consciousness is most constrained. The strong force is the binding that maintains form at maximum density, consciousness holding itself together in its most crystallized state.

The weak force governs transformation at that level, the dissolution and reconstitution that allows even the densest matter to change. Their range is short because maximum density means maximum locality. At the heart of the atom, there is nowhere else to reach.

The pattern: gravity relates form to formlessness. Electromagnetism relates light to form. The nuclear forces relate form to itself at maximum density. Three relationships, three scales, three aspects of the one process by which consciousness crystallizes, maintains, and transforms.

And Mercury, the dynamic principle, energy in motion? Mercury is not a separate force. Mercury is the relating itself. Energy is what moves between densities, what carries the interaction, what makes relationship dynamic rather than static. The forces are how Mercury operates through different combinations of Sulfur and Salt.

$E = mc^2$. Mercury = Salt $\times$ Sulfur^2. Energy equals the relationship between crystallized consciousness and the law that governs transformation. The forces are that relationship expressed at every scale.

This is not proven. It cannot be proven within the current framework because the current framework excludes consciousness by definition. But it is consistent. It is elegant. It is simple in the way real truths tend to be simple.

And it matches what practitioners have discovered through millennia of experimentation.

The Union

Light and Darkness are not opposed. They are poles of one reality.

The Nature of Light described consciousness descending into form, crystallizing into matter, forgetting itself in density. It mapped the

Tree from Kether to Malkuth, the formula of Sulfur/Mercury/Salt, the path of involution.

The Nature of Darkness described what holds the light: the ninety-five percent, the Ain that creates space, the Binah that gives form, the Abyss between manifest and unmanifest. It mapped the return, the dissolution of ego, the recognition of the ocean by the wave.

$E=mc^2$ unites them.

The equation describes the light's descent into matter and matter's release back into light. It describes the darkness as the space in which this transformation occurs, the c that governs, the law that allows. It describes consciousness as the unity underlying both, the thing that descends and the thing that ascends, the light that crystallizes and the awareness that recognizes.

Energy, matter, and the speed of light. Mercury, Salt, and Sulfur. Dynamic, crystallized, and the law that transforms between them.

The physicists have the equation. The mystics have the experience. The equation describes the experience. The experience proves the equation.

Not faith against science. Not religion against reason.

One truth, seen from two sides.

The grand unified theory has been written on chalkboards and t-shirts for over a century. It requires only the willingness to read it without the blinders that forbid consciousness from physics.

$E=mc^2$.

Consciousness in motion = Consciousness at rest $\times$ the law of transformation^2.

Everything is light, variously modified.

Part Six: The Implications

What This Means

If $E=mc^2$ is the formula of consciousness, then:

You are light. Not metaphorically. Actually. Your body is crystallized light, matter that was once energy that was once the primordial radiation of the Big Bang. The consciousness reading these words is the same consciousness that poured itself out into creation and is now recognizing itself in form.

Transformation follows law. The conversion between states is not arbitrary. c^2 governs. The alchemists did not discover this law; they described it. The physicists did not invent it; they measured it. The law operates whether you know it or not. Knowing it allows you to work with it consciously.

Density is not fixed. Matter becomes energy. Energy becomes matter. What seems solid can be released. What seems ephemeral can be crystallized. The body can be refined. Consciousness can be densified into talismans, released from attachments, circulated through channels that transform its quality.

The work is real. When you circulate light through the microcosmic orbit, you are running $E=mc^2$ in your own system. When you charge a talisman, you are crystallizing intention into matter. When you dissolve the ego's grip, you are releasing dense patterns back into fluid energy. The traditions discovered the formula through practice. Now you can see why the practices work.

The boundaries are permeable. Consciousness affects matter because consciousness and matter are not separate categories. The observer effect is real because observation is how consciousness interacts with the field of possibility. Intention shapes outcome because intention is consciousness directing itself. Magic works because magic is applied physics at the level where consciousness and matter meet.

What Changes

If this theory is taken seriously, not as philosophy but as operative truth, the implications reach everywhere.

Physics transforms. The measurement problem is solved: observation collapses the wave function because observation is consciousness interacting with the field of possibility. Dark matter and dark energy are reframed as the structure of consciousness that precedes and contains physical manifestation. The hard problem of consciousness dissolves entirely. There is no longer a question of how dead matter generates experience. Matter is experience at maximum density.

Technology reveals itself as material magic.

Consider what happens when a programmer writes code.

Code is pure information. Pattern. Logic. Intention expressed in symbol. It is Sulfur, consciousness with content, awareness shaped into specific form.

Electricity carries the code through circuits. Current flows, differential drives movement, energy propagates through conductive medium. It is Mercury, consciousness in motion, the carrier that moves pattern from one place to another.

Silicon executes the code. Matter arranged in precise structure, receiving the pattern, manifesting the result. It is Salt, consciousness at density, the material anchor that makes the operation real.

The program runs. Reality changes. Effects cascade into the world.

This is the alchemical formula executed through engineering. We have been doing material magic for decades. We call it technology. The server farm is a temple. The code is a spell. The electricity is the offering. The output is the manifestation.

Medicine integrates. If consciousness affects matter directly, placebo is not a confound to be controlled for. It is data about how healing actually works. The mind-body split underlying Western medicine collapses. Psychosomatic illness becomes consciousness affecting its own crystallized form, which is simply how things operate. Energy medicine, acupuncture, practices that work with subtle anatomy: these are no longer alternative. They work at less-dense levels of the same unified system.

Economics and politics shift. If consciousness shapes reality, and this capacity can be trained, then power structures built on controlling physical resources and information become less stable. You cannot monopolize consciousness the way you monopolize oil or data. Propaganda works by shaping the consciousness of populations to maintain certain consensus realities. If people understood that consensus reality is literally consensus, that observation shapes outcome collectively, they might become deliberate about what they observe, what they agree to, what they give attention to.

Religion loses its monopoly. Institutional religion can no longer claim exclusive access to the sacred. If consciousness is fundamental and $E=mc^2$ describes its operation, then the sacred is physics. You do not need a priest to intercede. You do not need doctrine to understand. The equation is available to anyone. But this does not kill spirituality. It validates it. The mystics were doing empirical research. The traditions encoded real discoveries. Science and spirituality are not opposites; they are the same investigation from different directions.

Part Seven: Why This Is Overlooked

The Suppression

If $E=mc^2$ already contains the grand unification, if consciousness is fundamental and the equation describes its operation, why has no one said so?

Some have. The mystics have said so for millennia, in their own languages. A few physicists have approached it: Schrödinger wrote on consciousness and Vedanta; Pauli collaborated with Jung on synchronicity; Wheeler pointed toward "it from bit" without completing the thought. They are ignored, marginalized, treated as having wandered outside their competence into mysticism.

The mainstream refuses to look. Not through conspiracy. Through something more effective: the immune response of a system protecting itself from destabilizing information.

How Suppression Works

Science is not a neutral method floating free of social context. Science is practiced by humans in institutions funded by governments and corporations with interests. What questions get asked depends on what research gets funded. What answers get accepted depends on what the community is willing to hear.

The materialist paradigm is not merely a scientific conclusion. It is a metaphysical commitment made before investigation begins. Consciousness is assumed to be emergent, secondary, reducible to matter. This assumption is not tested. It is the framework within which testing occurs. Evidence that contradicts it is not refuted; it is defined as "not science."

Physics departments do not fund consciousness research because it is "not physics," by a definition of physics that excludes consciousness a priori. Medical schools do not teach energy medicine because it is "not evidence-based," by standards of evidence designed to exclude the relevant data. Psychology separated from philosophy precisely to avoid these questions. The division of knowledge into disciplines functions to ensure certain questions fall between the cracks.

The reproducibility crisis in science reveals the fragility of the system. Studies fail to replicate at alarming rates. The response is not to question the paradigm but to blame individual researchers. The

71

possibility that consciousness might be involved in outcomes, that the observer affects the observed even in "objective" experiments, cannot be entertained because it would dissolve the framework that gives scientists their authority.

The Political Function

Materialism is not just wrong. It is useful to those who benefit from populations believing themselves to be powerless.

If you are a meat machine in a dead universe, you are fundamentally helpless. You require experts to interpret reality for you. You require institutions to organize your life. You require products to fill the void where meaning should be. You are a consumer, a patient, a citizen. Never a creator, never sovereign, never the source of your own experience.

This serves power. An atomized population of isolated individuals, each convinced of their own insignificance, is easy to manage. Consensus reality is manufactured through media, education, and the endless repetition of materialist assumptions. The boundaries of acceptable thought are policed not by censors but by social pressure, professional consequences, and the internalized conviction that certain ideas are crazy.

The Catholic Church suppressed heliocentrism not because it was false but because it threatened their authority. The earth at the center of the cosmos both reflected and reinforced the Church at the center of society. Modern institutions perform the same function with different content. Consciousness as epiphenomenal, humans as accidents, the universe as dead: this both reflects and reinforces a civilization built on extraction, control, and the denial of interiority to anything inconvenient.

But if consciousness is fundamental, if awareness shapes reality, if intention has physical effect, then authority becomes much harder to monopolize. You do not need a priest to intercede with God. You do not need a scientist to tell you what is real. The power is distributed to anyone who learns to work with it.

This is what they fear. Not that the theory is false. That it is true.

The Evidence They Buried

The evidence exists. It has simply been marginalized.

The Princeton Engineering Anomalies Research laboratory spent nearly thirty years documenting small but statistically significant effects of consciousness on random physical systems. The data was rigorous. The effects were real. The lab was closed and the research discontinued. Not because it failed. Because it succeeded in ways that could not be acknowledged.

The CIA's Stargate program investigated remote viewing for over twenty years. The final report, declassified in 1995, acknowledged "a statistically significant effect" that could not be explained by chance or methodological artifact. The program was cancelled. The official reason: not useful enough for intelligence purposes. The unstated reason: the implications were unmanageable.

Dean Radin, Rupert Sheldrake, and others continue to publish peer-reviewed research on consciousness effects. Their work is methodologically sound. It is also systematically ignored, dismissed, or attacked through means having nothing to do with the actual data. The immune response functions.

Thousands of years of contemplative practice across every culture, systematic investigation of consciousness through direct experience, is dismissed as "anecdote" by a science that has decided in advance that first-person data cannot count as evidence. The largest dataset in human history, the accumulated observations of meditators, mystics, and practitioners, is ruled inadmissible by methodological fiat.

The evidence is not lacking. The willingness to see it is lacking.

Why It Cannot Be Proved From Within

The current paradigm cannot be overturned from within because the paradigm defines what counts as proof.

If you assume consciousness is emergent from matter, then any experiment demonstrating consciousness affecting matter must be flawed, because such an effect is impossible by definition. The conclusion precedes the investigation. Evidence is filtered through assumptions that guarantee certain results cannot be found.

This is not science. It is theology wearing a lab coat. The materialist paradigm has become exactly what it accused religion of being: a closed system of thought that protects its core commitments by excluding contradictory evidence a priori.

The only way out is to change the assumptions before beginning. To start from the possibility that consciousness is fundamental. To design experiments that could detect this. To take seriously the data that already exists.

But this requires scientists willing to risk their careers, institutions willing to fund heresy, and a public willing to question assumptions they have absorbed since childhood. The immune response activates at every level.

What This Means For You

The theory will not be proved through official channels. The institutions that would need to validate it are the institutions that cannot afford to.

It will be proved the way the traditions always proved it: through practice, person by person, until the weight of lived experience becomes undeniable.

This is what the traditions have always offered. Not arguments to convince skeptics, but practices that transform practitioners. Not proof that satisfies the academy, but methods that produce results in the life of anyone who applies them.

You are the laboratory. Your experience is the data. The practices in this book are the experiments.

The materialists will continue to deny. Let them. Their denial is not your concern. Your concern is whether the work works, whether doing the practices produces the results the traditions promise.

If it does, you have your proof. Not proof you can publish, not proof that will convince those committed to not being convinced. But proof that matters: knowledge written in your own body, verified through your own experience, undeniable because you lived it.

This is how truth has always spread. Not from the top down, through institutional validation. From the inside out, through transformed lives.

The equation is $E=mc^2$. The proof is practice.

The Completion

The Nature of Light described descent: consciousness crystallizing into form, forgetting itself in matter.

The Nature of Darkness described return: the Abyss, the dissolution of ego, the recognition of the ocean by the wave.

The Unity describes the equation that governs both. The law that was always operating, the formula that physics discovered and forbade itself to understand.

$E=mc^2$ is not only physics. It is also metaphysics. It is also magic. It is the signature of consciousness operating in the physical world, the Rosetta Stone between science and spirit.

The proof is not in arguments that satisfy skeptics. The proof is in practice. The Work of Hands shows how. Your experience is the data. The work is remembering. The formula is how remembering operates. The practice is how you prove it to yourself.

Lux et Scientia, Unum

Light and Knowledge, One

The Work of Hands

The Theory Embodied in Practice

by Lux Indomita

The Nature of Light described what is. This document shows how those principles live in practice.

Not to teach techniques. You can find techniques anywhere. But to illuminate why the techniques work, so that what was rote becomes understanding, what was borrowed becomes yours, and what seemed like arbitrary tradition reveals itself as precise engineering.

When you see the theory operating in the practice, everything transforms.

On the Reality of the Work

Before we proceed, a word on what is real.

Is magic real? Are spirits real? Are the forces described in these pages actual things, or are they psychological constructs, symbolic frameworks, useful fictions?

The answer is yes.

When you believe something with complete sincerity, when you have convinced yourself utterly, it is real. Not metaphorically real. Real. Your neurology cannot distinguish between the vividly imagined and the externally verified. The map becomes the territory when the map is held with total conviction.

This is not weakness or delusion. This is how reality works for embodied consciousness. The boundary between inner and outer is more permeable than materialists suppose.

So: fake it until you make it, but understand that once you have made it, you are no longer faking. The spirits you contact may be external intelligences, or they may be archetypal forms arising from the deep psyche, or they may be something that renders that distinction meaningless. It does not matter. They respond. They act. They produce effects. That is real enough.

What does matter is this: the work requires your full participation. No god will act on your behalf while you watch. No spirit will take responsibility for your outcomes. You own every result, every consequence, every ripple that flows from your workings. This is karma in its original sense: action and the fruits of action.

Wishing accomplishes nothing. Begging accomplishes nothing. Even elaborate ritual accomplishes nothing if performed in the spirit of hoping someone else will do the work for you.

Magic requires that you step fully into authorship of your reality. You act. You accept the consequences. You take responsibility not just for your intentions but for everything that flows from them, including what you did not foresee.

This is not a burden. It is the price of power and the mark of maturity. The magician who will not own their results is not yet a magician. They are still a child asking the universe for favors.

Own it. All of it. Then the work becomes possible.

On Perception and Discernment

Spirits do not typically appear to physical sight. They do not materialize in the room like actors walking onto a stage, except in rare cases that require enormous energy and specific conditions.

What develops with practice is inner sight. The third eye, the subtle senses, the capacity to perceive what does not register on the physical retina. This perception is real. It is also internal, which does not make it less real. You are perceiving something, just not with your flesh eyes.

But do not mistake subtle for weak. Real contact is not ambiguous. When a spirit is present, you know. The temperature changes. The air feels thick or electric. Pressure builds against the circle. Something watches, and you feel the weight of its attention. It may speak, not always in words, but in impressions that arrive fully formed. The results in the days that follow confirm what the experience suggested.

If you have to wonder whether the contact was real, it probably was not. Faith is required at the beginning, when you are learning to perceive and your subtle senses are untrained. But faith is not required forever. Once the work is operating, it becomes very, very real. The dabbler may hit this once or twice by accident and dismiss it. The practitioner who persists will find it becomes consistent, reliable, unmistakable.

Do not expect Hollywood manifestations. But do not expect nothing either. Expect charge. Expect presence. Expect change you can feel in your body and verify in your life.

Imagination versus real contact:

Genuine contact surprises you. It contains information you did not know, perspectives you had not considered, answers to questions you had not consciously asked. Your own mind recycles what it already contains. Real contact brings something new.

Genuine contact is consistent over time. It does not contradict itself from session to session. It maintains coherent identity and purpose.

Your own imagination tends to tell you what you want to hear, or what you fear to hear. It inflates or deflates. It serves the ego's agenda of feeling special or feeling victimized.

Trustworthy spirit versus deceptive spirit:

Even when contact is real, the source may not be trustworthy. Spirits can lie. They can tell you true things to establish credibility, then mislead you when it matters. They can pass the basic tests while playing a longer game.

Watch for gradual boundary erosion. A spirit that respects your limits initially but slowly pushes for more access, more offerings, more dependence is not serving your interests.

Watch for whether following the guidance improves your life and character over time, or degrades them. Good counsel produces good fruit. If you are becoming more isolated, more grandiose, more unstable, more dependent, the source is not benevolent regardless of what it claims.

Watch for flattery. A spirit that tells you that you are special, chosen, more advanced than others, uniquely destined, is feeding the ego. It may be doing so deliberately to create attachment. Trustworthy spirits are more interested in the work than in your feelings about yourself.

This discernment takes time. Do not extend full trust quickly. Verify over months and years. A spirit willing to earn trust slowly is more likely to deserve it than one demanding trust immediately.

Spirit versus the Divine:

Contact with spirits, even trustworthy ones, is communication between beings. They have their own perspectives, limitations, agendas. They can help, teach, empower. They remain other.

Contact with the divine is something else entirely.

The divine is not a being among beings. It is the source itself, the ground of being, what the traditions call God, Dao, Ain Soph, Brahman, the One. Contact with the divine is not conversation. It is communion with what underlies all things, including you.

When Paul was struck down on the Damascus road, he was blinded and shattered. When Muhammad received the first revelation, he was seized, compressed, terrified, convinced he might be losing his mind. When Isaiah saw the Lord, he cried out that he was undone, unclean, annihilated before the holiness he witnessed. When Moses approached the burning bush, he could not look, could not stand on holy ground without removing his sandals, argued against the task because it was too much.

The pattern is consistent across traditions: genuine divine contact does not flatter. It overwhelms. It reveals your smallness against the infinite, or it dissolves the boundaries of self entirely into union with all that is. It is pure unconditional love, yes, but love so vast and so true that it burns away everything false. You come out transformed, often shattered and rebuilt, always humbled, usually with work to do that you did not choose.

You do not wonder whether contact with the divine was real. You are undone by it. The question afterward is not "did that happen" but "how do I live now."

There are gentler contacts that feel mediated: angels, saints, elevated beings serving as intermediaries. These can be more conversational, more bearable. They are real and valuable. But they are not the unmediated source.

Develop discernment through practice. Test what comes through. Be willing to be wrong. Over time, you learn to recognize imagination, to evaluate spirits carefully, and, if grace grants it, to recognize the difference between a messenger and the source of all messages.

The Formula Everywhere

Every tradition encodes the same formula: intention plus energy plus material anchor. Sulfur, mercury, salt. Will, force, basis.

The witch who dresses a candle with oil, speaks her will over it, and lights it at the proper moon phase is combining the three principles. Her spoken will is the sulfur. The energy comes from the burning candle, the lunar phase, her own raised emotion. The material anchor is the candle itself, the oil, the flame, the physical act of lighting.

The ceremonial magician who draws a circle, invokes divine names, traces symbols in the air, and charges a talisman is performing the same operation with more elaborate staging. More containers for intention. More sources of energy. More layers of anchoring. But the same formula underneath.

The prayer spoken with clasped hands and bowed head is also the formula. Intention directed toward the divine. Energy raised through devotion and longing. The physical posture anchoring the operation in matter.

The formula is universal. The costumes vary wildly. Once you see this, you can recognize magic anywhere and evaluate any technique by asking: where is the intention? Where is the energy? Where is the anchor? You can understand why some workings succeed and others fail. One of the three was weak or missing.

The Body in the Work

The body is not merely the platform from which you work. It is an instrument in the working itself.

The Nature of Light described the vertical axis running crown to root, the horizontal axis running through the heart and arms, the crossing point where transformation happens. These are operative in every act of magic.

When you raise energy for a working, you are running current through the vertical axis. The breath draws force up from the earth or down from above. It accumulates in the lower belly, rises to the heart, becomes available for direction. Without this circulation, you are trying to power the working from your surface reserves alone, which are thin and quickly spent.

When you project intention outward, you are using the horizontal axis. The heart transforms the raw energy with intention. The arms and hands direct it toward the target. Both hands can project, both can receive, but for most people the right side sends more naturally and the left receives more naturally. This is the default the healing and mesmeric traditions discovered independently. Your own body may differ. Learn what is true for you through practice.

When you receive, whether information through divination or energy in healing or communion with something greater, you are using the receptive capacity of the horizontal axis. The heart receives and interprets.

Your energetic state determines what is possible. Work from depletion and your workings will be weak regardless of technique. Work from overflow and even simple gestures carry force. Ground before you work. Center in the heart. Circulate energy to bring the reactor online. This takes minutes and multiplies the effect of everything that follows.

Why Timing Matters

The sky is not decoration. It is a clock that tracks real changes in the subtle environment.

Each moment carries a signature, a specific quality of energy determined by planetary positions, lunar phase, solar season. The ancients mapped these signatures through centuries of careful observation. They discovered that workings performed in alignment with celestial conditions succeed more readily than those performed against them.

This is not astrology as fortune-telling. This is astrology as engineering.

When you work for love on a Friday in the hour of Venus with the moon waxing and Venus well-dignified, you are timing your working to coincide with a moment when Venus-quality energy is maximally available in the environment. You are

catching a wave rather than paddling against the current. The same effort accomplishes more.

The election for a talisman captures a moment's signature and fixes it in matter. The talisman will broadcast whatever quality was present at the moment of its creation, for as long as it exists. Elect well and it broadcasts strength. Elect poorly and it broadcasts weakness or distortion. The stars at the moment of birth determine the nature of what is born. This is as true for talismans as for people.

Timing does not make a poorly designed working succeed. But it removes unnecessary resistance. The competent worker learns to read the sky not from superstition but from pragmatism.

What the Laws Describe

The traditional laws of magic are descriptions of how reality operates at the level of pattern and information. They are as reliable as gravity.

Correspondence describes the fractal nature of reality. Patterns repeat across scales because each level contains all other levels within it. The solar system mirrors the atom. The body mirrors the cosmos. A symbol shares structure with what it symbolizes. When you work with a symbol, an image, a model, you are working with something that resonates at the same frequency as what it represents. Affect one and the other responds.

Similarity describes resonance. Like attracts like because similar patterns vibrate at similar frequencies. This is why the talisman works. It broadcasts a specific signature, and that broadcast resonates with similar influences in the environment. Like a tuning fork that causes other tuning forks of the same pitch to vibrate in sympathy, the talisman's signal calls to what matches it. Those influences are drawn toward the source of the resonance. The talisman does not contain the power. It calls the power through sympathetic attraction.

This is also why inner state matters for outer results. To attract love, cultivate the frequency of love within yourself. You become the talisman. Your state broadcasts its signature and draws corresponding influences toward you.

Contagion describes information entanglement. Things that have touched have exchanged pattern. They remain correlated even after separation. This is why personal effects link to their owners. The hair, the photograph, the beloved object carry the signature of the person they came from. This is also why you should be careful what you leave behind, what gifts you accept, what exchanges you make. Connection is created through contact, and connection can be used.

Names describe compression. The true name of a thing encodes its full pattern in speakable form. Speaking the name with energy and intention unpacks that pattern into presence. This is why names of power are vibrated, not merely

spoken. The vibration adds energy to the pattern. The name provides the address. Together they invoke what the name names. To name is to have access.

Invocation and the Spell

Invocation and spell work illuminate the polarity principle from opposite directions.

In invocation, you draw a force into yourself. You create internal space, emptiness shaped to receive a specific quality, and that quality flows in to fill you. The divine name vibrated, the god-form assumed, the surrender of ordinary identity, all serve to create the receptive space. You become the cup. What you invoke pours in.

This is the receptive pole. Yin. You empty yourself to be filled.

In spell work, you project a force outward. You accumulate charge, shape it with intention, and release it toward a target. The raised energy, the focused will, the physical gesture of release, all serve to send the pattern forth. You become the wand. What you have charged fires outward.

This is the projective pole. Yang.

The complete magician works both directions. Invoke first, bringing the force into yourself. Then project, sending it forth shaped by your intention. This is why ceremonial structures often begin with invocation and end with the specific working. You fill the cup, then pour from it.

The Stone itself embodies this unity. It receives and projects simultaneously, the perfect balance of polarities, neither empty nor overflowing but both at once. The magician who has formed the Stone no longer alternates between invocation and projection. The two become one continuous movement, breathing in and breathing out as aspects of the same breath.

Until then, work both poles consciously. Learn to receive. Learn to project. Feel the difference. Then feel how they connect.

The Talisman Illuminated

A talisman is crystallized intention radiating continuously.

The election captures a moment of optimal celestial alignment. That moment's signature is caught and fixed the way a photograph catches light. The talisman does not create the planetary influence. It captures what was present at the moment of its making.

The materials resonate with the desired quality. Gold resonates with solar energy because gold and sun share signature. Silver with moon.

Copper with Venus. Iron with Mars. The metal is an antenna tuned to a specific frequency.

The symbols inscribed are compression keys. The seal of Jupiter contains Jupiter's pattern in geometric form. Inscribing it programs the talisman with that information. The symbols are not decoration. They are code.

The consecration ritual combines sulfur, mercury, and salt. Intention is clarified and focused. Energy is raised through invocation, through breath, through concentration. The charge is fixed in the material basis through definite acts of completion.

Once complete, the talisman broadcasts its signature continuously. Like a bell that has been struck, it rings at its particular frequency. That frequency resonates with similar influences in the environment, calling them, attracting them toward the source of the signal. Like calls to like, and like responds by moving toward the caller.

The operator's development determines how much charge the talisman can hold and how clearly it broadcasts. A weak operator makes a weak talisman regardless of technique. The internal state is an ingredient that cannot be substituted.

Protection

Before reaching outward, establish safety.

Grounding connects your energy body to the earth before and after every working. Visualize roots extending down from your base into the earth. Excess energy drains away. Stability flows up. The earth can absorb anything.

Centering gathers your awareness to your core before you begin. Do not work while scattered, distracted, or emotionally volatile. Find the center point in your heart. Operate from there.

Shielding maintains a baseline energetic boundary. A sphere of light surrounding you, permeable to what you welcome, impermeable to what you do not. Simple and consistent beats complex and occasional.

Banishing clears the space before and after significant workings. Before, to remove whatever influences might interfere. After, to clear whatever was drawn and is no longer needed. Learn one banishing ritual and use it until it is second nature. The specific form matters less than consistent use.

These are not advanced techniques. They are basic hygiene. Neglecting them is performing surgery without washing your hands.

Working With Spirits

The traditions describe hierarchies of non-physical intelligences: angels, planetary spirits, elementals, the dead, and others. They can be contacted and worked with. This is real, and it is dangerous in ways that demand respect.

Approach with caution. These are intelligences with their own natures, agendas, and interests. Some are benevolent. Some are indifferent. Some are predatory. You cannot tell which by how they present themselves. Assume nothing.

Work through proper channels. The hierarchies exist for good reason. Contacting a planetary spirit through its angel and intelligence is safer than direct contact. The hierarchy provides structure and protection. Going around it removes that protection.

Maintain boundaries. You are the operator. You decide what you will and will not do, what access you will and will not permit. A spirit that pressures you past your boundaries, demands more than agreed, flatters excessively, threatens subtly, or creates urgency is not acting in your interest. Trust your discomfort. End contact that feels wrong.

Be careful with thanks and gifts. To thank a spirit can be to acknowledge debt. The words "thank you" imply that something was received and that obligation exists. In spirit dealings this can be binding. A debt acknowledged is a debt owed, and spirits may collect in ways you did not anticipate.

Instead of thanks, offer praise. "You have done well." "Your power is evident." Praise acknowledges performance without creating obligation.

To accept a gift from a spirit is to accept connection. The gift carries the spirit's signature. It creates contagion. It may create obligation that escalates over time. Gifts freely given are rare.

Structure exchanges carefully. Negotiate before the work begins. State what you offer and what you expect. State the limits. State when the arrangement ends. Be precise. Spirits are literal and will exploit ambiguity.

Everybody gets paid. Offerings serve two purposes: resonance and fuel. Things that match the spirit's nature create resonance, making contact clearer. Things that carry energy provide fuel, powering the work and compensating the spirit for its effort.

Planetary spirits appreciate offerings that correspond to their planet. Solar spirits receive gold, yellow candles, frankincense, offered on Sunday in the sun's hour. Lunar spirits receive silver, white candles, jasmine, offered on Monday in the moon's hour. This creates resonance through similarity.

But the offerings also provide energy. The candle burning releases force. The incense dissolving gives something up. The food or drink offered is consumed at subtle levels. The spirit gains something real. So does the working.

Attention itself is offering. Regular devotion, a maintained altar, spoken prayers. Attention is energy. Consistent attention over time builds relationship and provides steady fuel.

Whatever you agree to, fulfill completely. A broken agreement with a spirit is worse than no agreement.

License to depart. Formally end the contact and close the channel. Without this, the connection may persist, and what comes through an open channel is not always what you invited.

You are not the only target. If a spirit wishes to harm you and cannot reach you directly, it may reach toward those you love. Family, friends, animals, anyone connected to you is potentially a vector. Your protections must extend to those within your sphere. The consequences of error may fall on those who did not choose the risk.

On Demons Specifically

Avoid them.

This is not superstition. This is practical counsel from those who have worked both paths and seen where each leads.

Demons can do nothing for you that you cannot accomplish through your own development or through work with non-demonic spirits. Nothing. Whatever they offer, there are other ways to reach it.

What demons offer is shortcut. What they cost is hidden and compounds over time.

They attach. They do not complete a transaction and depart. They remain present, bound to your attachments, your desires, your outcomes. They hide in your wounds, in your desperation, in your grasping. These are their food. They feed on wanting. The arrangement that seemed like a bargain becomes parasitic and deepens over time.

They obscure the heart. The work of opening, of dissolving ego, of transcending duality, becomes vastly harder with demonic attachment. They have interest in keeping you bound, wanting, feeding them. A closed heart serves them. Your liberation does not.

There is no completion on their path. No peace. No satisfaction that lasts. Only deeper entanglement and mounting cost.

The warnings in the old grimoires are observations from practitioners who documented what they saw. The demons do what they promise. They also do what they do not mention, and that is where the price accrues.

Stay away. Whatever you think you need from them, find another way.

Healing as Circulation

The healer channels energy from source to target. Channel, do not spend. If you push from your own reserves, you deplete yourself. If you draw from the infinite source and direct it through yourself, you are a conduit. The river flows through you without diminishing you.

The channel runs through the heart because the heart transforms. Energy drawn from above descends to the heart center, is shaped by love and intention, and flows out through the hands. The healer's open heart is not sentimental nicety. It is operative. A closed heart cannot heal. It can only push energy, which may or may not help.

Clearing before filling reflects understanding of blockage. Often illness is stagnation. Adding energy to a blockage feeds it. Clear the obstruction first, then fill with vital force.

Distance is not a barrier because similarity and contagion operate regardless of proximity. A photograph, a name, a clear mental image creates sufficient link. The energy follows the connection.

Divination as Reading Pattern

Divination works because of correspondence.

A spread of cards, a cast of stones, a chart of the heavens all reflect the pattern of the situation they are asked about. The micro mirrors the macro. What appears random is not random. It is correlated with the pattern you are asking about.

Through the act of asking, you connect your question to the system. Through the moment of casting, the arrangement that manifests corresponds to that moment's pattern. And that moment's pattern is the pattern of your question, because you asked in that moment. Chance is what we call correspondence we have not yet understood.

This is why state of mind matters. If you are scattered, your question is scattered, and the answer reflects scatter. If you are clear, the answer reflects clarity.

This is not reading a fixed future. Patterns can be changed. Divination shows the pattern as it stands and the trajectory it implies if nothing intervenes. Weather forecasting, not prophecy. Useful for planning, useless for fatalism.

The reader's skill lies in perceiving what the symbols show without projecting hope or fear onto them. The symbols mean what they mean. Reading clearly

requires the same clarity that all magical work requires.

Daily Practice

Transformation is built through daily repetition, the way water shapes stone.

The daily practice matters more than the occasional elaborate working. Consistency matters more than intensity. What you do every day determines what you become.

Morning alignment. Upon waking, before the day scatters you, take five minutes. Ground to the earth. Center in the heart. Run the orbit to bring the vessel online.

Evening clearing. Before sleep, release what accumulated. Ground again. Let anything foreign or unbalanced drain away. Sleep clean.

Regular banishing. Once a day or at minimum once a week, clear your space.

Devotion. Address the divine daily. Not begging for outcomes but aligning with what is higher. This opens the heart and maintains orientation toward the Great Work.

Service. Give without expectation of return. Small kindnesses count. This dissolves ego more reliably than any technique.

Observation. Watch yourself. Notice your states, your reactions, your patterns. Self-knowledge is the foundation of transformation. You cannot change what you do not see.

The dramatic workings have their place. But the daily practice is where transformation happens. It is the slow pressure that shapes the stone.

When Things Go Wrong

Things will go wrong. This is not failure. It is learning.

Sometimes burnt fingers are the best teacher. You will make mistakes, misjudge situations, overreach your capacity, attract attention you did not want. This is part of the path. The question is not how to avoid all error but how to recover from error wisely.

Go low and go slow. When you encounter difficulty, back off. Reduce the intensity and complexity of your work. Return to basics. Ground more. Banish more. Stabilize before you push forward again.

Do not be afraid to stop entirely for a time. If magic is creating problems, switch to devotion. Prayer without intent, worship without agenda, surrender to the

divine without asking for anything. This cools what has become overheated. It reconnects you to sources larger than yourself. When you return to active work, you return from a more stable foundation.

If devotion is creating problems, obsession or inflation or disconnection from ordinary life, switch to practical magic. Ground the energy in specific, concrete workings. Come back to earth. Balance the vertical with the horizontal.

Having help matters enormously. A teacher who has walked the path can see what you cannot see about yourself. A lineage or tradition provides egregore support, the accumulated power and protection of all who have practiced that way before you. A genuine connection to divinity, not just theoretical but felt and reciprocal, means something larger than you is watching out for your development.

The traditions emphasize lineage for good reason. Not because independent work is impossible, but because it is harder and more dangerous. When things go wrong, the independent practitioner has only their own resources. The practitioner embedded in living tradition has backup.

If you lack lineage, cultivate divine relationship directly. Devotion to a god, an angel, a saint, a bodhisattva, whatever face of the divine calls to you. Ask for protection and guidance. Offer your practice in service. Something that sees further than you can see will begin to look out for you. This is not superstition. It is one of the most practical things you can do.

Specific remediation is beyond the scope of this document. What to do when you have attracted something you cannot banish, made an agreement you cannot fulfill, or sustained damage you cannot heal yourself requires specific diagnosis and specific response. Find help. A competent practitioner, a priest, a healer, someone who can see what is happening and address it. Pride that prevents seeking help has ended more magical careers than any demon.

The path is long. Setbacks are not endings. Learn what the setback teaches, recover your footing, and continue.

The Limit of Practice

All of this is preliminary.

The techniques work. Understanding why they work makes them work better. Mastery of practical magic is genuinely useful and attainable.

But technique alone does not complete the Great Work.

The vertical axis is cleared by practice. The heart is opened by living. The third stage is not achieved by any technique however refined. It is received by those who have made themselves ready through purification, through service, through love, through the dissolution of everything false.

Use these understandings. Become skillful. And remember what they are for. The Stone forms in the heart. All else is preparation.

Per Opera, Lux

Through Works, Light

The Practice of Light

Technical Instructions for the Work

by Lux Indomita

"The physical body is the crucible or athanor into which we must pour our alchemical elixir of the Stone. It must be strengthened and fortified, and purified so that it may be of proper use under much higher temperature and pressure."

— Lady Mercury

Preface: What This Document Is

The Nature of Light explains what light is. The Nature of Darkness explains what darkness is. The Unity synthesizes them into a single framework. The Work of Hands explains ethics and discernment.

This document explains what to do.

These are the practical instructions for internal alchemy, energy cultivation, and magical operation. They derive from fifteen years of practice. They are technical. They are specific. They are meant to be used.

Nothing here is merely symbolic. The orbit is real. The third eye is real. The qi is real. The entities are real. What you do with this information will have real effects in your life.

Begin only when you are ready. Proceed with appropriate caution. What follows is not a metaphor.·

A Note on Simplicity

Traditional systems are often elaborate, and often beautiful. Daoist alchemy prescribes specific postures, precise breathing, visualization stages unfolding over years. Ceremonial magic requires memorized rituals, exact timing, particular tools. These traditions carry genuine wisdom. Their practices work. Many find home in them.

The elaboration serves real functions: reverence through difficulty, filtering for commitment, community through shared practice. But much of the complexity exists because traditions preserved what worked without always understanding why. When you lack the mechanism, you compensate with structure. The structure works, but the practitioner may not know which elements are essential and which are scaffolding.

This document illuminates why the practices work, not just how. When you understand the mechanism, you gain discernment. You can honor tradition while seeing what it actually does.

If you have found home in a traditional system, keep it. Understanding the mechanism deepens appreciation. But if you have struggled with elaborate systems without results, this offers another approach. The instructions here are simple because the mechanisms are understood. Simplicity is not lack of depth. It is depth clarified.

The grounding technique requires placing Yi in the earth and allowing yin to rise. That is the mechanism. The orbit completes when both poles are held in awareness. The third eye opens through gentle Yi placement. The formula for magic is Sulfur plus Mercury plus Salt equals Stone.

Do the practices. See what happens. Use what works.

Part One: The Foundation·

The Three Treasures

The Daoist tradition speaks of three treasures: Jing, Qi, and Shen. These are not abstract concepts. They are substances, forces, modes of consciousness that you can learn to perceive and work with directly.

Jing

Jing is the most dense. It is essence, vitality, the foundational life force stored in the body. Think of it as your inherent bodily resilience, the deep reserve that determines how quickly you heal, how well you resist illness, how much capacity you have for sustained effort. Jing concentrates in the lower body, in the kidneys and sexual organs, but it is not merely sexual energy. It is base vitality itself, of which sexual energy is one expression. Jing is the battery. It is the raw material from which higher energies are refined. It accumulates slowly through rest, nutrition, and healthy living. It depletes rapidly through stress, illness, overwork, and excessive sexual release.

If you are exhausted, depleted, unable to concentrate, unable to feel energy at all, your jing is low. Rebuild it before attempting any advanced work. This means sleep, food, reduced stress, and allowing the body to recover. There are no shortcuts.

Qi

Qi is finer than jing but denser than shen. It is energy in motion, the breath of life, the current that animates. Where jing is the deep reserve, qi is the active circulation, more etheric, more immediately available, more responsive to direction. Qi circulates through the body via channels the acupuncturists mapped. It can be gathered from the earth, from the air, from food, from the sun. It can be directed by attention. Where the mind goes, qi follows.

The microcosmic orbit circulates qi. Qigong and taichi cultivate it. Proper breathing gathers it. Emotional regulation prevents its scattering. Qi is the fuel in active use. Jing is the battery; qi is what the battery produces. If jing is low, qi production suffers. If qi is scattered through emotional chaos or improper breathing, the system cannot function.

Shen

Shen is the finest of the three. It is spirit, consciousness, the light itself. Shen resides in the heart and in the third eye. When shen is clear, you perceive clearly. When shen is disturbed, reality seems distorted, thoughts are confused, perception is unreliable.

The three treasures transform into each other through the process of internal alchemy. Jing rises and refines into qi. Qi rises and refines into shen. Shen, at its highest, returns to the void. This is the vertical axis of the work. ·

The Dantian

The dantian is the cauldron. It is the center, the furnace, the storage vessel, the place where transformation occurs.

Locate it: approximately two inches below the navel and two inches inward, toward the center of the body. Not on the surface. Not at the skin. In the core, the center of gravity, the place where all the forces meet.

The dantian is not a pole of the circuit. The poles are the third eye above and the perineum below. The dantian is what forms between them. It is yin qi, accumulated through grounding and reception. You do not activate the dantian directly. You build it by grounding into the earth and allowing yin to fill you. Over time, this accumulated earth qi becomes the cauldron itself.

Think of it this way: the circuit runs between third eye and perineum. The dantian is the reservoir that forms when you run the circuit while grounded. It is storage, not source. It is effect, not cause. Build it through grounding, and it becomes the foundation for all further work. ·

Grounding

Grounding is not metaphor. It is not 'feeling connected to nature.' It is the actual establishment of an energetic connection between your body and the earth.

To ground:

Position matters less than presence. You can stand, sit, or lie down. The physical posture is scaffolding; the work is done by Yi.

Place your Yi in the earth. Not at the floor. Not at your feet. In the earth itself, deep, in the fiery core, in the molten heart of the planet. Let your awareness sink down through rock and water and magma until it rests in that immense reservoir of yin energy.

Then relax. Let go. Stop efforting.

What happens next is not something you do. It is something you allow. The earth qi rises naturally into you. You do not pull it; it comes. The yin fills the vessel the way water fills a hole. You simply opened the connection by placing your awareness there. The earth does the rest.

The sensation is unmistakable once you feel it: being embraced by the earth. Held. Supported. Filled with something dense, cool, stable. Some feel heaviness in the legs and feet. Some feel warmth spreading upward. Some simply feel solid, rooted, unshakeable. The specific sensation varies; the quality of stability is consistent.

Once established, the connection persists for a time even after you withdraw active attention. You have opened a channel. It remains open until you close it or until distance and distraction gradually let it fade.

Practice this until you can establish it reliably. When properly grounded, you are harder to move physically. You have access to energy that does not deplete your own reserves. You have a foundation from which to work.

Without grounding, all other work is unstable.

You will run current without a reservoir. You will deplete your own jing. You will burn out. Ground first. Ground always. ·

The Microcosmic Orbit

The microcosmic orbit is the fundamental energy circuit of the body. It runs up the back and down the front, connecting the major energy centers in a continuous loop.

The pathway:

Starting at the perineum (the point between genitals and anus), energy rises up the spine. This is the Du Mai, the Governing Vessel, the yang channel. It passes through the sacrum, the lumbar spine, between the shoulder blades, up the neck, over the crown of the head, down the forehead to the upper palate.

At the upper palate, the circuit requires a bridge. This bridge is the tongue. When you place the tongue on the roof of the mouth, just behind the front teeth, you complete the connection between the yang channel and the yin channel.

From the palate, energy descends the front of the body. This is the Ren Mai, the Conception Vessel, the yin channel. It passes through the throat, the heart center, the solar plexus, the navel, and down to the perineum, completing the circuit.

The power source:

The orbit runs on jing. This base vitality, concentrated at the perineum, is what the circuit circulates and refines. Without jing, there is nothing to move. This is why depleted practitioners get no results. The tank is empty.

As the orbit runs, jing rises up the spine, refining at each energy center. When it reaches the third eye, it meets the descending light and is purified further. This refined energy descends the front channel to the dantian, where it accumulates. Over time, this accumulated essence forms what the Daoists call the pearl, and what the alchemists call the first stone.

The perineum is the gate. By gently engaging these muscles (similar to stopping urination, but subtler), you can redirect sexual energy into the spinal channel when arousal arises. This is not clenching. It is a light energetic lift, barely perceptible. This technique increases the fuel available for circulation.

How to practice:

This is the traditional sequential practice. It clears the channels, develops Yi, and builds the habit of circulation. It is preparatory work, not the completion technique. That comes later, in the Opening and Closing section. But the preparation is essential. Without clear channels and developed Yi, the completion technique will not work.

Sit comfortably with spine straight. Place tongue on the upper palate. Breathe naturally. Bring attention to the perineum.

As you inhale, draw attention up the spine, from perineum to sacrum to lumbar to thoracic to cervical to crown. Do not force. Simply move attention. The qi follows.

At the crown, let the inhale complete. Feel the top of the head, the connection to the heavens, the incoming light.

As you exhale, draw attention down the front, from forehead to throat to heart to solar plexus to navel to perineum. The circuit completes.

Repeat. Again and again. Let the circulation become automatic. Eventually you will feel the energy moving on its own, the orbit running continuously. The technique for initiating this self-sustaining flow, the method that transforms practice into awakening, is described in the Opening and Closing section below.

This is the foundation of all internal work. Everything else builds on this circuit. ·

Sexual Energy: A Clarification

The traditions speak of retaining sexual energy, and this has been catastrophically misunderstood by certain communities. Let me be direct: retention does not mean permanent celibacy. It does not mean never ejaculating. It does not mean you will become immortal by refusing to have sex.

The people on certain forums who believe they will achieve immortality through permanent retention are, to put it plainly, deluded. They have taken a practical technique and turned it into a neurotic obsession. They are not achieving enlightenment. They are achieving frustration and often psychological damage.

Here is what the teaching actually means:

Sexual energy is one expression of jing, the base vitality. When you ejaculate, you expend some of that vital reserve. This is natural, healthy, and necessary for human life and connection. The question is not whether to expend it, but whether to expend it wisely.

When you are depleted, when you are exhausted, when you have been running energy hard for magical work, you have less jing to spare. During these times, retention allows the reserves to rebuild. It is like not spending money when your bank account is low. This is practical, not religious.

When you are healthy, rested, with reserves built up, sexual expression with a loving partner is one of the great pleasures and powers of human existence. The polarity between partners generates energy. Done consciously, sex can be a magical act that generates more than it consumes.

The orbit allows you to circulate sexual energy rather than simply expelling it. Even during sex, you can run the circuit, draw the energy up the spine, refine it. This is the basis of sexual cultivation practices in both Daoist and Tantric traditions. It does not require abstinence. It requires awareness.

Ejaculate when you are full and the exchange serves connection and pleasure. Retain when you are depleted and need to rebuild. Use discernment. Do not make an ideology out of biology. ·

Yi: The Mind-Intention

Before discussing the pearl, understand Yi.

Yi is often translated as intention, but this is incomplete. Yi is the mind-will, the focused direction of consciousness that moves energy. Where Yi goes, qi follows. This is not metaphor. It is mechanism.

In qigong and internal alchemy, Yi is the key. The physical movements are scaffolding. The breath is support. But the actual work is done by Yi, by the focused direction of awareness.

When you run the microcosmic orbit, you are not merely imagining energy moving. You are placing Yi at successive points along the circuit. The qi follows because that is the nature of qi: it goes where attention goes.

When the third eye opens and you project across the room, you are extending Yi. When you shock someone with qi, you are projecting Yi with force. When you heal, you are directing Yi with intention into the target's energy body.

Yi is also how you move consciousness out of the body. The senses are not fixed to the physical form. They are information, and information can be relocated. By moving Yi, by placing your sense of awareness in a location outside the body, you begin the process of astral projection. The third eye is the organ that facilitates this. But Yi is the operator.

All the visualizations in Western magic, all the movements in qigong, all the breath work in pranayama, these are methods for training and directing Yi. The technique is the container. Yi is the content.

If you do the movements without Yi, you are exercising. If you do the movements with Yi, you are doing alchemy. ·

Building the Pearl

The pearl is the first stone. It is accumulated refined essence stored in the dantian. It is not built overnight. It is built over months and years of consistent practice.

What the pearl does:

The pearl is storage. Without it, you have only the energy you generate moment to moment. With it, you have a reservoir. You can run more current. You can sustain practice longer. You can survive experiences that would deplete someone without reserves.

The pearl is also stability. When you have built a pearl, your energy does not scatter as easily. Your emotions are more stable. Your attention is more focused. Your health is more robust.

The pearl is the foundation for all higher work. You cannot safely open the third eye without it. You cannot cross the Abyss without it. The vessel must be fortified before higher pressures are applied.

How to build it:

Run the orbit daily. Cultivate jing through retention and proper living. Gather earth qi through grounding. Breathe fully and properly. Reduce emotional volatility that scatters energy.

Over time, the accumulated refined essence collects in the dantian. You may feel it as warmth, as fullness, as a sense of something solid and stable in your core. The sensation is unmistakable once it develops.

Do not try to rush this. The pearl builds at its own pace. Force creates instability. Patience creates foundation.

Part Two: The Third Eye·

The Radio

The third eye is a radio. This is not metaphor. It is the most accurate description of what it does.

A radio has two functions: it receives signals, and it transmits them. The third eye does both. It is a transceiver, operating at frequencies beyond the physical senses.

When closed or dormant, you perceive only the physical world. The radio is off. When opened, you perceive the subtle: energies, entities, currents of force that move beneath and behind the visible. The radio receives.

When you project intention, when you work magic, when you influence at a distance, you transmit. The radio broadcasts.

Most people go through life with the radio off. They see only the physical layer. They miss the ninety-five percent of reality that operates at frequencies they cannot detect.

Those who open the third eye begin to pick up what was always there. The astral plane overlaps the physical completely. Yesod mirrors Malkuth down to the smallest particle. The information is present at every point. You simply were not tuned to receive it.·

The Worker of Magic

The third eye is not merely a passive receiver. It is the worker of magic. It is the organ through which magical operations actually function.

When you visualize a sigil, hold it in your mind, and charge it with intent, where does that happen? In the third eye.

When you see the pentagram you trace hanging in the air, glowing, present on the astral overlapping the physical, what sees it? The third eye.

When you project qi across the room and someone reacts, what aimed the projection? The third eye directed it. Yi moved through the third eye to the target.

When you scry and images form, when you receive transmission from intelligences, when you see entities manifest in your temple space, the third eye is the organ of perception.

Magic becomes vastly easier when the third eye is open. What was effortful becomes natural. What required elaborate ritual can be done with a thought. The difference is not in the magic itself but in the capacity to perceive and direct the forces involved.

This is why so many practitioners struggle. They do the rituals, speak the words, make the gestures, but their third eye is closed. They are operating blind. The magic may still work, crudely, through sheer repetition and accumulated force, but it is like trying to paint with your eyes shut.

Open the third eye, and you see what you are doing. You see the energy gather. You see the sigil form. You see the entity arrive. You see the effect take hold. Then you can adjust, refine, direct with precision. Then magic becomes what it is supposed to be: an art.·

Location and Mechanism

The third eye is located in the center of the head, behind and slightly above the point between the eyebrows. It corresponds physically to the pineal gland, but it is not the pineal gland. It is the energetic structure that the pineal gland anchors.

In Qabalistic terms: the crown is Kether, the divine source, the point where infinite light enters the system. The third eye is Chesed, where that light becomes workable, where the magician operates. You do not work at Kether. You receive from it. You work at the third eye.

The traditional Daoist teaching runs jing upward: sexual energy rises from the base, refines through each center, and meets the descending light at the third eye. This works. Millions of practitioners over millennia have achieved results this way.

What I found works better: start at the third eye. Contact the light first. Then bring the light down to meet the jing. Ground at the base, pull from heaven. This is the lightning flash, divine power descending through the planes while you are rooted in earth. You become the conduit between above and below.

The traditional approach asks you to push energy upward against gravity, against the natural descent of light. My approach rides the lightning down. Both complete the circuit. One is harder than it needs to be.

Foundation still matters. The jing must be there, built through proper living, rest, cultivation. Without jing, there is nothing for the light to meet. Without the pearl, there is no reservoir to sustain the connection. You need both poles. But you can start from either end, and starting from the light is faster.

People who force the third eye open through drugs or intense meditation without foundation have problems. They turn on the radio without building the power supply. They receive, sometimes overwhelmingly, but they cannot sustain. They cannot control. They often cannot close it.

Build the foundation. Run the orbit. Generate the pearl.

When these are established, the third eye opens naturally, sustainably, controllably. Then you are not overwhelmed by what you receive. Then you can transmit without depleting yourself. Then magic becomes possible in the full sense. ·

As Receiver

When the third eye is open and receiving, it picks up information from the subtle planes. This information arrives as images, impressions, knowings, sometimes words. The quality varies. Some signals are clear; some are distorted. Some sources are reliable; some are not.

The clarity of reception depends on the state of your shen, the development of your pearl, and your ability to quiet the mind enough to hear what is being transmitted.

Think of it as tuning. When you are calm, centered, with energy running clean, you tune precisely. The signal comes through clear. When you are anxious, scattered, depleted, the tuning drifts. You get static. You pick up interference. You may receive, but you cannot trust what you receive.

The noise-to-signal ratio is a real concern. Not everything that comes through is accurate. Not everything that appears is what it claims to be. Discernment requires not only an open third eye but a trained one, one that has learned to filter, to evaluate, to recognize the difference between genuine transmission and random noise. ·

As Transmitter

When the third eye projects, it broadcasts your attention, your intent, your consciousness into the field. This is how remote influence works. This is how you can affect people and situations at a distance. This is how you make yourself visible to entities.

When you place your attention somewhere and project through the third eye, that place receives your consciousness. If you project strongly, with intent, with qi behind it, the effect is tangible. People feel it. Animals feel it. Sensitive observers can see it.

This is how you can shock people across the room. This is how you can influence outcomes. This is how you can send a spell to its target. Yi moves through the third eye, carrying the intent, powered by qi.

This is third eye projection in action. The magician sees the outcome, directs Yi through the third eye, and reality bends to match the pattern broadcast.

This is not metaphysics. This is mechanism. The third eye broadcasts information and energy into the informational substrate of reality. The substrate responds. What we call manifestation is the physical world aligning with the pattern you transmitted.

When the third eye is open and the operator knows how to use it, magic is simply a matter of clarity, power, and aim. See what you want. Direct Yi. Project with force. The rest follows.·

The Danger

When the third eye opens, you become visible to everything that can see at that frequency. You are broadcasting. You are also receiving indiscriminately until you learn to filter.

Opening the third eye without foundation is like turning on a radio and a beacon simultaneously. You hear everything. Everything can see you. Not everything that approaches is friendly.

This is why the orbit comes first. This is why the pearl matters. This is why protection is not optional. The foundation stabilizes. The storage provides reserves. The protection creates boundaries.·

Opening and Closing

You can learn to open and close the third eye at will. This is essential for sanity and safety.

A Note on This Technique:

What follows is not in the classical texts. The Secret of the Golden Flower, the Wuzhen Pian, Liu Yiming, all describe moving Yi sequentially around the circuit, not holding two poles simultaneously. The components are classical: Yi as operator, light as confirmation, spontaneous circulation as goal. But the synthesis is mine.

I spent years with published methods. Paid for courses. Read the classics. Practiced daily. The channels cleared. The Yi developed. But the circuit never completed. The orbit remained something I did rather than something that ran. Then this technique came through, and within days what years had not accomplished simply happened. The circuit closed. The energy flowed on its own.

The classical approach works eventually for some. Those who achieve spontaneous circulation through extreme stillness are unknowingly achieving dual-pole awareness long enough for completion. What follows is more direct, but not a shortcut around foundation. Without grounding, Yi, qi sensitivity, and meditative capacity, this will not work. The jing must be there. The channels must be partially clear. But for those with foundation who have struggled, this may complete the circuit.

No specific timeline. Attempt when ready. Succeed when capable. If it does not work, return to foundation and try later.

The sequential orbit practice, moving attention up the spine and down the front, remains valuable. It clears channels and develops Yi. Consider it preparation. What follows is completion.

To open:

The key is Yi, mind-intention, placed lightly on the third eye point. Not forced concentration. Not straining. Not pushing energy anywhere. Just gentle awareness, like resting your attention on a distant sound without grasping at it.

Bring your Yi to the third eye point, the space in the center of the head, behind and slightly above the point between the eyebrows. Do not push. Do not force energy there. Simply be aware of that location. Hold your attention there lightly, the way you might notice warmth on your skin without focusing intently on it.

You will know you have found the correct spot when you see the light.

This is not metaphor. Not visualization. Not imagination. Real light. It may appear as a point, a glow, a field of luminosity in your inner vision. It may be faint at first, barely perceptible. But it is actual light perceived through the activated third eye, not constructed by the mind. When you see it, you have found the pole. This is confirmation that you have made contact.

A clarification: this confirmation light is not the Golden Flower. The classical texts describe luminous phenomena, 'silver moon in heaven,' 'great earth as a world of light,' representing later development, the pearl becoming radiant after months or years of practice. The confirmation light is simpler: Yi has found the upper pole. It is the beginning, not the fruit. The confirmation light says 'you are here.' The Golden Flower says 'you have arrived.'

Once the third eye pole is activated through this light-contact, bring the light down. The traditional teaching runs energy up from the base. What I found: start with the light, bring it down to the jing. Ride the lightning flash rather than pushing against it.

From the third eye, draw your awareness down the front of the body, throat, heart, belly, all the way to the perineum, the very base of the spine. Bring the light to the jing. You are grounded in earth. You are pulling from heaven. You become the circuit.

Now hold both poles simultaneously.

Yi remains lightly at the third eye. Yi also rests at the perineum. When you hold both poles at once, lightly, without strain, the energy begins to circulate on its own.

The snake wakes up. It descends from the third eye, down the front channel, reaches the perineum, rises up the spine, and returns to bite its own tail at the third eye. This is what the orbit feels like when it completes. Not energy pushed around a track, but a serpent finding its own mouth.

You do not push the energy around the orbit. You do not visualize it moving. You open the circuit by holding both ends in awareness, and the energy flows of its own nature. Like completing an electrical circuit: you connect the terminals, and the current runs. Force is not required. Presence at both poles is what initiates the flow.

This is the technique most practitioners miss. They try to push energy up the spine through willpower. They visualize movement and wonder why nothing happens. The orbit initiates not through force but through simultaneous awareness at both poles. Yi in two places. Gentle contact at each. Then the system runs itself.

If you have built sufficient qi through foundational practices, grounding, breathing, cultivation, the opening is unmistakable. Something clicks on. Perception shifts. You begin to see or sense what was previously invisible. The transceiver activates. You are now both receiving and, if you direct it, broadcasting.

To close:

Withdraw Yi from the third eye. Release the dual-pole awareness. Bring all attention down to the dantian and let it rest there, single-pointed. Draw any excess energy down the front channel and store it in the lower center.

Ground firmly into the physical. Feel your body, the weight, the breath, the sensations of the material world. If needed, stamp your feet, eat something heavy, touch the earth directly. Pull your awareness fully into Malkuth, into dense matter, into the body.

Closing is as important as opening. If you leave the third eye open constantly, you will exhaust yourself. You will be overwhelmed by input. You will lose the ability to function in ordinary reality. The subtle planes do not turn off; you must learn to tune away from them when the work is done.

Learn to open for work and close for rest. Learn to filter what you receive. Learn to choose what you broadcast.

Common Errors:

Forcing with concentration: Creates headaches and false phenomena. The light comes through gentleness. If you are clenching or pushing, relax. The light appears when you stop trying to make it appear.

Pushing or visualizing the orbit: Visualization is training, not mechanism. The orbit runs when both poles are held simultaneously. You do not need to imagine energy traveling.

Holding only one pole: Many focus on the third eye and neglect the perineum, or vice versa. The circuit requires both. Split your Yi.

Mistaking imagination for perception: Visualized light feels constructed, effortful, controlled. Perceived light appears to you, sometimes unexpectedly, with a quality of givenness. If uncertain, you are probably imagining. Keep practicing. When the real perception comes, you will know.

Expecting immediate drama: The third eye opens gradually. The light may be faint at first. Do not dismiss subtle phenomena. Dramatic openings often indicate insufficient foundation. Slow and steady builds sustainable capacity.

Part Three: Magical Operation·

The Formula

All magic operates by the same formula:

Sulfur + Mercury + Salt = Stone

Sulfur is intent, the idea, the mental pattern you wish to manifest. It is consciousness-with-content. It is what you want to create.

Mercury is energy, the qi, the force that carries the intent. It is consciousness-in-motion. It is what powers the working.

Salt is physical action, the embodiment, the material anchor. It is consciousness-at-density. It is what grounds the working into manifestation.

When you combine a clear mental intention with sufficient energy and anchor it with physical action, you create a stone. Something crystallizes. Something manifests. The working completes.

This is why visualization alone rarely works for most people. They have Sulfur but not Mercury. They have intent but no energy behind it.

This is why energy work alone rarely produces specific results. They have Mercury but not Salt. They have power but no anchor into form.

This is why physical rituals without presence do nothing. They have Salt but not Sulfur. They have the action but no consciousness driving it.

All three must combine. All three must align. Then creation happens.

In practice:

Decide what you want to create or accomplish. Get clear. Make the mental image specific. This is the Sulfur.

Gather energy. Run the orbit. Pull from the earth. Build charge in the dantian. Feel the power accumulating. This is the Mercury.

Take a physical action that symbolizes and embodies the result. This could be a ritual gesture, a spoken word, a written symbol, a specific movement. Something that represents the manifestation in material form. This is the Salt.

At the moment of combination, release. Let the intent carried by the energy anchor into the action and project outward. Do not grasp at the result. Let it go to do its work.

This is magic. It is not more complicated than this. It is also not less.·

Working with Intelligences

The planetary forces have consciousness. They can be communed with, invoked, petitioned. The traditions call them gods, angels, spirits, intelligences. The name matters less than the relationship.

Protocol:

Approach with respect. You are addressing something far older and more powerful than yourself. Do not demand. Do not threaten. Do not grovel. Speak as you would to a wise and powerful teacher whose help you need.

Use the proper forms. The traditions have established names, symbols, invocations, offerings. These are not arbitrary. They are protocols that have been proven to work, established over centuries of contact. Use them.

Be clear about what you are asking. Vague requests get vague responses. Specific requests can be specifically answered. Know what you want before you call.

Give something in return. The relationship is reciprocal. Offerings, devotion, attention, service: these maintain the connection. Taking without giving damages the relationship and can generate unfavorable consequences.

Close properly. When the working is complete, license the spirits to depart. Thank them for their presence. Close the gates you opened. Do not leave doors hanging open.

With elementals:

Elementals are simpler beings than the planetary intelligences. They have less individual will, more nature. They can be helpful, but they require specific handling.

Do not speak first. Let them approach. Let them initiate. If you greet them before they greet you, you may create an obligation you do not want.

Do not thank them. Thanking creates a debt, a bond. Acknowledge their assistance without gratitude that binds.

Be clear about terms. Elementals follow instructions literally. What you say is what they do. Ambiguous commands produce ambiguous results.·

Protection

Every magical operation should begin and end with protection. Every practitioner should maintain baseline protective practices daily.

The Lesser Banishing Ritual of the Pentagram:

This ritual is public, well-documented, and effective. Learn it. Practice it daily. It clears the space, establishes boundaries, and reinforces your authority in your own territory.

The LBRP is not merely symbolic theater. It is an alchemical furnace. It applies the formula. It makes you the stone. Daily practice builds the vessel, fortifies the boundaries, develops the energetic musculature needed for more advanced work.

Circle casting:

Before any working that invokes external forces, cast a circle. The circle defines the boundary between inside and outside, between what is yours and what is other. Only what you invite may enter. What enters must depart when the working ends.

The circle is not just a line on the ground. It is an energetic structure. Build it with intent (Sulfur), power it with energy (Mercury), anchor it with physical marking (Salt). Make it real.

Licenses to depart:

When a working is complete, dismiss what you have called. Do not assume they will leave on their own. Do not leave the connection open. Speak the dismissal clearly.

Some entities do not want to leave. Some will test the boundary. If you have built the circle properly, if your will is firm, they must depart. If your will wavers, if your authority is weak, they may linger.

This is why foundation matters. This is why the pearl matters. Weak will cannot command. Strong will, backed by genuine capacity, is respected by all beings.

Part Four: The Awakening·

When the Snake Bites Its Tail

There is a moment when the orbit stops being something you do and becomes something that is. The circuit completes. The snake bites its tail. The system runs continuously.

This is awakening.

Not metaphorical awakening. Not 'I feel more spiritual now.' Actual, functional awakening. The third eye opens not as an occasional glimpse but as a persistent state. You perceive the subtle as naturally as you perceive the physical. You run energy without effort. You know things you have no normal way of knowing.

When this happens, everything changes.

You become visible in a new way. You operate under new rules. Powers become available that were not available before. Responsibilities emerge that did not exist before.

The warning is real: 'Having the Stone of any one realm places an unprepared being in incredible and mortal danger. Suddenly new rules of the game and higher principles apply. You are subject to the mercy of new beings who are far more advanced than you.'

This is true. Awakening is not graduation. It is matriculation. You have entered a new school where you are once again a beginner. Act accordingly. ·

The Danger of Intensity

The system can run too hot. When too much energy flows through channels not yet capable of handling it, damage occurs.

Signs of running too hot:

Insomnia. Racing thoughts that will not stop. Inability to close the third eye. Seeing things constantly, without rest. Physical symptoms:

headaches, pressure in the head, heat that will not dissipate. Emotional extremes: euphoria, terror, rage that comes from nowhere.

What to do:

Ground. Hard. Feet on actual earth. Pull the energy down out of the head, out of the chest, down into the dantian, down into the earth. Let the earth take the excess.

Stop practice. Do not run the orbit. Do not meditate. Do physical things. Eat heavy foods. Exercise. Sleep. Let the system cool down.

Time. The channels need time to adapt to higher currents. What is too much now will be manageable later, once the capacity develops. Do not rush this process.

Pushing through is not strength. Pushing through damages the system. The vessel must expand gradually or it cracks. Respect the limits of the body.·

The Return

After awakening, after running hot, after the system stabilizes: the return.

You come back to ordinary life. You still have a job, a family, bills, dishes. The cosmic consciousness that glimpsed its own nature still has to show up for meetings and buy groceries.

This is not a failure. This is the point.

The Work is not escape from matter. The Work is the exaltation of matter. The wave knows it is ocean and continues to wave. The embodied consciousness knows it is universal and continues to embody.

This is the mission: 'To save and redeem and exalt matter. Prometheus was the first to bring the divine spark of light into regular matter... We are the Saviors to be of Matter and the Fallen, and our great work is to bring to pass the creation of the stone and the exaltation and restoring of Divinity to Matter.'

Not transcendence out. Transcendence through.

Spirit fully incarnate in flesh, operating as flesh, transforming flesh from within. This is the Stone. This is the Grail. This is why we are here.·

Integration

The awakening must integrate. The extraordinary must become ordinary, reliable, repeatable, normal.

This takes time. Years, perhaps. The initial opening is dramatic. The integration is gradual. The temptation is to chase the dramatic. The work is in the gradual.

Run the orbit daily, but gently. Maintain protection without paranoia. Use the sight when needed; rest when rest is needed. Build the pearl slowly, steadily, patiently.

What was touched remains. The path stays open. It rests, recovers, waits for the vessel to be ready again. When ready, it returns. Not overwhelming, but accessible. Sustainable. Yours.

·

Closing: Be Cautious and Wise

Humility is not optional.

"There is always a bigger fish."

"If you have the stone of the Wise, you must not show it and protect it at all costs."

"Be thou cautious and wise."

This is practical advice from beings who see more than we can. The path is real. The powers are real. The dangers are real. Build foundation before reaching for heights. Protect what you develop.

The Work continues. What you need will come when you need it. Trust the process. Trust the teachers who prove trustworthy. Trust yourself.

The snake has bitten its tail before. It will bite again.

Until then: practice, ground, circulate, build.

This is the Work.

Do it.

Fac et Intelliges

Do and You Will Understand

Colophon

✦ ✦ ✦

Lux Indomita is one person.

One person, acting alone. No organization. No coven. No council. No degrees, no credentials, no ordination, no formal training in theology or ministry. Only what was lived through and what came out the other side.

And if I can do all this... just think of what You can do.

There is no guru behind this curtain. No prophet to follow. No leader who can grant you access to what is already yours.

Anyone who claims to be Lux Indomita is a liar.

Anyone who claims to speak for Lux Indomita is a liar.

Anyone who claims special knowledge of their identity is a liar.

If someone uses these words to gather followers, to build a hierarchy, to place themselves between you and the divine, **KNOW** they serve the same old master in new robes.

They are Clergy of the Demiurge. Walk around them.

You do not need them. You never did.

We are all Lux Indomita, and that includes You.

The Unconquerable Light literally Lives within YOU.

That is the whole point. The Name belongs to No One because it belongs to All. Take it. Use it. Pass it on. You do not need permission. The Sacred is Yours.

This Work is released into the World, ownerless. It is Fruit from the Tree. It was never Mine to keep.

The light is not owned.

The light is not led.

The light is not contained.

The light simply is.

And so are you.

www.ingramcontent.com/pod-product-compliance
Lightning Source LLC
Chambersburg PA
CBHW060330050426
42449CB00011B/2716